MUSIC OF THE UNITED STATES OF AMERICA

Richard Crawford, Editor-in-Chief
Mark Clague, Executive Editor
Victoria von Arx-Zak, Assistant Editor

---

1 Ruth Crawford: Music for Small Orchestra (1926); Suite No. 2 for Four Strings and Piano (1929)
Edited by Judith Tick and Wayne Schneider

2 Irving Berlin: Early Songs, 1907–1914
Edited by Charles Hamm

3 Amy Beach: Quartet for Strings (in One Movement), Opus 89
Edited by Adrienne Fried Block

4 Daniel Read: Collected Works
Edited by Karl Kroeger

5 The Music and Scripts of *In Dahomey*
Edited by Thomas L. Riis

6 Timothy Swan: Psalmody and Secular Songs
Edited by Nym Cooke

7 Edward Harrigan and David Braham: Collected Songs, 1873–1896
Edited by Jon W. Finson

8 Lou Harrison: Selected Keyboard and Chamber Music, 1937–1994
Edited by Leta E. Miller

9 Harry Partch: Barstow—Eight Hitchhiker Inscriptions from a Highway Railing at Barstow, California (1968 Version)
Edited by Richard Kassel

10 Thomas Wright "Fats" Waller: Performances in Transcription, 1927–1943
Edited by Paul S. Machlin

Thomas Wright "Fats" Waller

Performances in Transcription
1927–1943

Edited by Paul S. Machlin

Recent Researches in American Music • Volume 41

Music of the United States of America • Volume 10

Published for the
American Musicological Society
by

A-R Editions, Inc.

Middleton, Wisconsin

Published by A-R Editions, Inc.
Middleton, Wisconsin

Printed in the United States of America

ISBN 0-89579-467-5
ISSN 0147-0078

Frontispiece: Fats Waller at work, ca. 1940, photographer unknown, catalog title "ICON Waller, Fats no. 1"; reproduced by permission of the Music Division, The New York Public Library for the Performing Arts, Astor, Lenox, and Tilden Foundations.

Copyright permission statements appear on p. v.

Publication of this edition has been supported by a grant from the National Endowment for the Humanities, an independent federal agency.

∞ The paper in this publication meets the minimum requirements of the American National Standard for Information Sciences—Permanence of Paper for Printed Library Materials, ANSI Z39-48-1984.

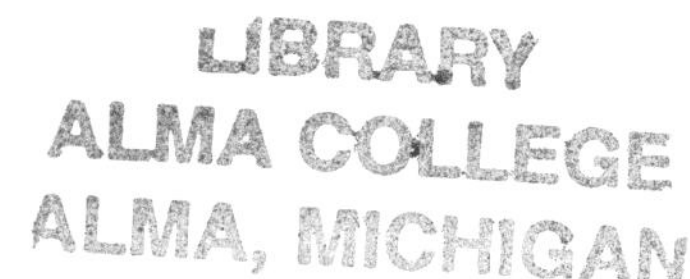

Grateful acknowledgment is made for permission to use the following:

Ain't Misbehavin', music by Thomas "Fats" Waller and Harry Brooks, words by Andy Razaf
© 1929 (Renewed) EMI Mills Music Inc., Chappell & Co., Razaf Music Co. and The Songwriters Guild of America
International Copyright Secured / All Rights Reserved / Used by Permission
Warner Bros. Publications U.S. Inc., Miami, Florida 33014 and Hal Leonard Corporation, Milwaukee, Wisconsin 53213-0819

Gladyse, by Thomas "Fats" Waller
© 1929 (Renewed) Chappell & Co. (ASCAP)
International Copyright Secured / All Rights Reserved / Used by Permission
Hal Leonard Corporation, Milwaukee, Wisconsin 53213-0819

Honeysuckle Rose, music by Thomas "Fats" Waller, words by Andy Razaf
© 1929 (Renewed) EMI Mills Music Inc., Chappell & Co., Razaf Music Co. and The Songwriters Guild of America
International Copyright Secured / All Rights Reserved / Used by Permission
Warner Bros. Publications U.S. Inc., Miami, Florida 33014 and Hal Leonard Corporation, Milwaukee, Wisconsin 53213-0819

I Ain't Got Nobody, music by Spencer Williams, words by Roger Graham
© 1916 Craig & Co.
Used as part of the public domain (entered 1982)

I Can't Give You Anything But Love, words and music by Dorothy Fields and Jimmy McHugh
© 1928 (Renewed) EMI Mills Music Inc.
Rights for Extended Renewal Term in U.S. controlled by Aldi Music Co. and Ireneadele Publishing Company
International Copyright Secured / All Rights Reserved / Used by Permission
Warner Bros. Publications U.S. Inc., Miami, Florida 33014

I'm Crazy 'Bout My Baby, music by Thomas "Fats" Waller, words by Alexander Hill
© 1931 (Renewed) Edwin H. Morris & Company, a division of MPL Communications, Inc.
International Copyright Secured / All Rights Reserved / Used by Permission
Hal Leonard Corporation, Milwaukee, Wisconsin 53213-0819

It's a Sin to Tell a Lie, by Billy Mayhew
© 1936 (Renewed) WB Music Corp.
International Copyright Secured / All Rights Reserved / Used by Permission
Warner Bros. Publications U.S. Inc., Miami, Florida 33014

Rusty Pail Blues, by Thomas "Fats" Waller
© 1927 (Renewed) Chappell & Co. (ASCAP)
International Copyright Secured / All Rights Reserved / Used by Permission
Hal Leonard Corporation, Milwaukee, Wisconsin 53213-0819

That Does It, attributed to Thomas "Fats" Waller
Used by permission of the Thomas "Fats" Waller Trust, M. William Krasilovsky, trustee and the Clifford Morris Collection, part of the World Music Archives of the Olin Library at Wesleyan University (Middleton, Connecticut), donated by Clifford Morris and organized by Herman Dean and Ed Kirkeby.

Waiting at the End of the Road, by Irving Berlin
© 1929 (Renewed) Irving Berlin
International Copyright Secured / All Rights Reserved / Used by Permission
Hal Leonard Corporation, Milwaukee, Wisconsin 53213-0819

Musical sketches in Waller's hand from the personal collection of Victor Amerling; used by permission.

Dedicated with affection and gratitude to Sue, Greg, and Erica.

CONTENTS

FOREWORD

Music of the United States of America (MUSA), a national series of scholarly editions, was established by the American Musicological Society (AMS) in 1988. In a world where many developed nations have gathered their proudest musical achievements in published scholarly form, the United States has been conspicuous by its lack of a national series. Now, with the help of collaborators, the AMS presents a series that seeks to reflect the character and shape of American music making.

MUSA, planned to encompass forty volumes, is designed and overseen by the AMS Committee on the Publication of American Music (COPAM), an arm of the society's Publications Committee. The criteria foremost in determining its contents have been: (1) that the series as a whole reflect breadth and balance among eras, genres, composers, and performance media; (2) that it avoid music already available through other channels, duplicating only where new editions of available music seem essential; and (3) that works in the series be representative, chosen to reflect particular excellence or to represent notable achievements in this country's highly varied music history.

The American Musicological Society's collaborators in the national effort that has brought MUSA to fruition include the National Endowment for the Humanities in Washington, D.C., which has funded MUSA from its inception; Brown University's Music Department in Providence, Rhode Island, which provided the project's original headquarters; the University of Michigan School of Music, where MUSA now makes its home; A-R Editions, Inc., the publisher, on behalf of AMS, of the MUSA series; and the Society for American Music, which, through its representative to COPAM, has provided advice on the contents of MUSA.

Richard Crawford, Editor-in-Chief

PREFACE

Since the 1950s, when I first heard Waller on disc thanks to my father's enthusiasm (and his collection of 78 rpm recordings), his performances have never failed to intrigue and energize me. Waller's good humor in performance is infectious, his swing and elegance captivating. *Thomas Wright "Fats" Waller: Performances In Transcription* stems from my profound admiration for the work of this remarkable musician as well as from my involvement with his recorded output over the course of two decades. In many ways, this volume may be read as a companion to my first study of his work—*Stride: The Music of Fats Waller* (Twayne Publishers, 1985). It is intended to provide a view of Fats Waller's contributions to American music that is both coherent and in some measure representative of the multifaceted nature of his career.

The repertoire presented in this volume has been chosen to reflect the range of his performance styles (stride, swing, comic, parodic), his principal instruments (piano and pipe organ), his singing, and some of the various sonic contexts in which he recorded (solo keyboard, solo vocal, duet, and small ensemble). The performances chosen range from 1927 to 1943, chronicling the stylistic developments of his professional career. In addition, the volume offers paired transcriptions of performances of the same tune. This pairing affords the opportunity to examine how Waller treats the same material under different sets of circumstances. Such comparisons help clarify the nature of Waller's musical gestures and ideas, and they attest to his fertile imagination as a composer as well as his improvisational skill.

At a basic level, Waller's recordings can be divided into two groups—performances of his own compositions and performances of works by other composers. Other more specific categories, however, based on the different kinds of recording experiences he logged in the studio, allow for more useful and precise distinctions. Waller's alternate takes show that he constantly varied his interpretations, even in consecutive performances of the same piece played on the same instrument. This volume sets forth alternate takes of solo performances on each of Waller's two principal instruments, piano ("Gladyse," Transcriptions 1a/b) and pipe organ ("Rusty Pail Blues," Transcriptions 2a/b). In addition, at one 1929 session (29 August), Waller recorded alternate takes of the Irving Berlin song "Waiting At The End Of The Road" (Transcriptions 3a/b) on pipe organ and on piano. These versions show Waller, on a single occasion, adapting the same material to the expressive possibilities inherent in his two chosen instruments.[1] In another session, Waller's two takes of the song

[1]On at least a few sessions at the height of his career Waller also recorded an instrumental and a vocal version of a song consecutively (with "His Rhythm" on 29 November 1936 and 9 April 1937, and as a soloist on pipe organ in England on 28 August 1938; see Brian Rust, *Jazz Records 1897–1942*, 5th Revised and Enlarged Edition [Chigwell, Essex, UK: Storyville Publications, n.d. (ca. 1982)], 1629–30, 33).

"I Can't Give You Anything But Love" (Transcriptions 4a/b), recorded once with another singer and again on his own, demonstrate how deep the stylistic gulf between his versions of a single song could become. In the duet he signifies on his partner's performance with biting intensity, unleashing an equally satirical wit in his own chorus. In the solo take, by contrast, his approach to the song verges on tenderness.

Not all of Waller's multiple performances of individual songs were recorded at single sessions. A pair of performances of the same song recorded at different times in his career can suggest changes in Waller's musical approach over time, revealing a broad range of inventiveness. Four such pairs are included here. In two sets of these pairs, Waller used the same instrumentation (solo piano/vocal for "I'm Crazy 'Bout My Baby," Transcriptions 5a/b, and solo piano for "Honeysuckle Rose," Transcriptions 6a/b). In two other pairs, Waller used different instrumentation for each performance (solo piano and piano/vocal for "Ain't Misbehavin'," Transcriptions 7a/b, and solo piano and pipe organ for "I Ain't Got Nobody," Transcriptions 8a/b). Finally, one recording ("That Does It," Transcription 9, from a group of homemade acetate recordings of Waller performing his songs from the musical *Early to Bed*) can be correlated with Waller's handwritten sketches of the same material, thus documenting the kinds of alterations Waller made in realizing his own draft score.

It is my hope that this edition will serve performers, scholars, and readers who are interested in Waller's music making. To that end, the edited transcriptions include precise tempos, dynamic levels, articulations, pedaling, and other expressive markings. Detailed performance commentary for each transcription supplements the notation, and occasional footnotes supply alternative readings of ambiguous pitches or passages. However, it is important to note that the recordings from which the transcriptions were made remain essential to achieving a full understanding of Waller's style. Though the transcriptions provide complete and basically self-sufficient renderings of his performances, the recordings directly document the feel and subtle nuance of Waller's playing and singing that notation cannot fully represent.

The three sections of the edition—the essay, the transcriptions and accompanying notes, and the apparatus—are interrelated and complementary. The essay brings to the surface aspects of Waller's composing and performing that are illustrated by the transcriptions, the notes expand on the observations in the essay, and the apparatus provides details on the sources as well as a guide to the notation. The method of transcription is also described in the apparatus.

Acknowledgments

During my work on this volume I have benefited beyond measure from the expertise, interest, encouragement, support, and generosity of a great number of colleagues and friends. After my father, my friend Stephen Nuthall directed me towards Waller studies by presenting me with the first RCA France Waller Memorial boxed set of LP recordings over a quarter century ago; he is responsible, then, for providing me the opportunity to sharpen my awareness of the riches in Waller's work and for suggesting that his performances were worthy of greater scrutiny than they had hitherto received.

Three MUSA executive editors—the sum total of those who have held that position—have had jurisdiction over this edition in one way or another. Wayne Schneider solicited the original proposal, and I am grateful to him for championing it and shepherding it through the vetting process, for continuing to reassure me during the inevitable delays, for helping to secure its eventual approval, and for commenting on early versions of the essay and on the transcription of "Rusty Pail." Jeffrey Magee continued this tradition of encouragement. Mark Clague has overseen the crucial editing of the entire manuscript—music and text—in its final stages. It would be difficult to imagine a more meticulous yet sympathetic editor, particularly one who is endowed with extensive reserves of patience and an enviably buoyant sense of humor.

Two sections of the essay were presented in preliminary form as papers at the annual meetings of the Society for American Music (1996) and the International Musicological Society Congress (1997). They were also read by Gavin Jones, Margaret McFadden, and Michael Broyles; for their detailed and incisive critiques, which strengthened my early work considerably, I am most grateful. I am also happy to thank my sister Jennifer Machlin, who is a superb editor and helped me restructure and bring clarity to the introduction. MUSA's editor-in-chief Richard Crawford read and edited several drafts of the essay in detail, raising important questions that influenced my thinking. Ingrid Monson provided illuminating commentary on signifying. Her expertise helped clarify my analysis, and I am grateful to her for suggesting ways to summarize Henry Louis Gates's definition.

Nothing substantial in music research could ever be accomplished without the aid of music librarians. Vincent Pelote, Edward Berger, and Dan Morgenstern, all of the Institute of Jazz Studies at the Newark campus of Rutgers University, have consistently allowed me to take advantage of their encyclopedic knowledge of jazz history and discography; in their generosity and good will they are emblematic of their profession. James Farrington (at that time, music librarian at Wesleyan University) first alerted me to Wesleyan's acquisition of the Clifford Morris Collection of Waller recordings on tape, and gave me essentially unlimited access to it. His assistant Jennifer Hadley also helped by making dubs of crucial items in the collection. For assistance at the Music Division of the New York Public Library, I am grateful to Susan Sommer and Frances Barulich. Wayne Shirley, at the Library of Congress, helped me find my way along the twisted path of the sale and purchase transactions that constituted the often bizarre history of copyright possession for many of the compositions included in this volume.

David Joyner and Michael Golden, both accomplished jazz pianists, scrutinized early drafts of some of the transcriptions; their corrections and suggestions materially improved the accuracy of several knotty moments. Victoria von Arx-Zak, MUSA's assistant editor, checked over the final drafts of the transcriptions and made many helpful suggestions. James Dapogny, editor of Jelly Roll Morton's piano works for the Smithsonian, reviewed several sample transcriptions and made suggestions to clarify the notation. I would also like to thank fellow MUSA volume editor Lee Orr, along with James Hammond of the University of New Orleans, who provided guidance in refining the organ transcriptions.

Victor Amerling deserves special recognition in these acknowledgements. Requiring no formal arrangements whatsoever, he entrusted to me his entire collection of Waller sketches—a uniquely valuable repository of original work by Waller. Further, he allowed me to retain the collection since he first brought it to my attention in 1994. His generous support for this project has greatly facilitated my work and measurably enhanced the edition.

I also owe a particular debt of gratitude to my two research assistants, T. Casey McCullough (Colby '96) and Kurt Kelley (Colby '99). Each spent a summer transforming my handwritten transcriptions into computer documents using the Finale notation program. Both demonstrated an enviable mastery of the skills necessary to manipulate this complex program so that the elusive elements of Waller's playing could be rendered in print in the notational forms I had designed for them. In the process, they raised many questions, leading to corrections and changes that have enhanced the edition, though this often meant an even greater expenditure of time and energy on their parts. In these especially laborious tasks they were both ideal collaborators.

Several colleagues at Colby College provided other kinds of assistance that must be acknowledged with gratitude: Cheryl Townsend Gilkes, John D. McArthur Associate Professor of African-American Studies and Sociology; Peter Ré, Professor Emeritus of Music; Margaret E. Libby, slide curator of the Art and Music Library; and Barbara Russo, administrative secretary of the music department.

For hospitality on many trips to New York City to conduct research, I thank my friends Bob and Marcia Marafioti, Stephanie and Roger Traub, and Jay and Susan

Evans Sterling. I am also grateful for the helpful counsel of Daniel Hughes, Felix Springer, and Robert Hayes.

During the 1995–96 academic year, when much of the work on this volume was undertaken, I was supported in part by a National Endowment for the Humanities Fellowship for College Teachers; I also received funding from the Humanities Grants Committee at Colby College.

My wife Susan Sterling and our children Greg and Erica, to all of whom this book is dedicated, share my love of Fats Waller and understand (as only true aficionados can) my fascination with his music. Greg and Erica, as a result of countless hours of overhearing Waller's performances emanating from my study, have learned to tolerate my often overweening enthusiasm for Waller with good humor and have become as captivated by his wit as I have. Sue has been engaged with the project since its inception. Reading and critiquing the manuscript with a scrupulously impartial eye, she has prompted me to consider carefully the implications of my words. Responding to my often fragmented ideas about the music with insights of her own, she has helped me to rethink and revise wherever necessary. And always she has been a source of warm and vital encouragement. Throughout the lengthy tenure of my work on this project, the love of these three wonderful people has sustained me and made my family a welcome refuge from the labors of this project. For this and for being who they are, they have my boundless affection and gratitude.

Paul S. Machlin

"WALTZING THE RUMBA"

Waller's Transformative Art

WALLER'S CAREER

Thomas Wright "Fats" Waller (21 May 1904–15 December 1943) attained widespread recognition as a pianist early in his professional life, but his developing career did not follow a single trajectory. He engaged in an exceptionally broad range of creative endeavors (perhaps more than any other jazz musician of his time) and excelled in each. His constant schedule of live engagements—on radio in the early 1930s, in clubs, on tours, and in shows throughout the decade—resulted in both an enhanced technique and an assured, relaxed approach to performance. The evidence documenting Waller's many activities is vast. It includes the hundreds of 78 rpm discs as well as unreleased takes he made for the Victor Talking Machine Company[1] (among others), airchecks of radio shows, and a few brief but memorable appearances on film. This recorded legacy illuminates Waller's most immediately recognizable qualities as a performer: his propulsive swing, his brilliant technique, the inventiveness of his improvisations, the infectious enthusiasm of his musical persona, and his humor. It also helps explain his influence, which extended not only to other pianists (notably Count Basie and Art Tatum) but also well beyond his immediate contemporaries. Indeed, even trumpeter and bandleader Dizzy Gillespie, whose contributions to the development of bebop in the 1940s were crucial, acknowledged Waller as a source of inspiration, recognizing that Waller's humor was an integral component of his art: "I am serious about my music, but I like to have fun, too. Fats Waller always had fun, and he was my main man."[2]

Waller's parents, Edward and Adeline, married in Virginia in 1888, and shortly thereafter migrated to New York City.[3] Thomas was the fourth of their five surviving children.[4] By the time of his birth, the family had moved from Greenwich Village, where

[1]The Victor Talking Machine Company grew out of Berliner Gramophone, taking over the patents of inventor Emile Berliner (1851–1929). Reflecting a trend toward consolidation in the recording and radio industries, the Victor Company merged with the Radio Corporation of America in 1929 to form RCA Victor. For the purposes of this essay, the company will be referred to consistently as the Victor Company.

[2]Interview with Dizzy Gillespie on the CBS network program "60 Minutes," 13 December 1981.

[3]Maurice Waller and Anthony Calabrese, *Fats Waller* (New York: Schirmer Books, 1977), 1–2. This biography, by Waller's son, together with Ed Kirkeby's reminiscence, *Ain't Misbehavin': The Story of Fats Waller* (New York: Dodd, Mead & Company, 1966; reprinted New York: Da Capo, 1975), are the most reliable published sources for basic biographical information about Waller's early years.

[4]Maurice Waller notes that Adeline gave birth to eleven children, of whom six died in infancy or childhood (Waller and Calabrese, *Fats Waller,* 2). According to Kirkeby, who refers to the Waller family Bible as a source of information about Waller's siblings, Adeline gave birth to twelve children (Kirkeby, *Ain't Misbehavin',* 4, 7). The wording of Kirkeby's account, however, suggests a possible miscalculation on his part; eleven children is probably the correct number.

they had become affiliated with the Abyssinian Baptist Church, first to West 63rd Street, following the relocation of the Church to West 40th Street, and ultimately to 107 West 134th Street in Harlem. This odyssey paralleled the general move of African Americans in New York City to northern Manhattan.

According to family history, Waller's mother Adeline was deeply musical, and music was woven into the fabric of daily life in the Waller household. The family acquired a piano around 1910,[5] and the young Thomas must have begun to teach himself almost immediately. Though he apparently had some basic formal instruction in music as a child, both privately and at school,[6] most of his early musical experiences seem to have been the result of a keen ear and a predisposition to listen closely and attempt to recreate what he heard. In addition to experimenting with the piano at home, Waller played harmonium to accompany his father's streetcorner preaching. (Shortly after their move to Harlem, the family's religious affiliation had changed to the Refuge Temple on West 133rd Street, and Edward Waller became a lay preacher for their new faith.[7])

During the first half of the 1920s, as Waller advanced from adolescence to young adulthood, his work in music provided a well-rounded apprenticeship for his multifaceted career. He taught himself certain technical aspects of playing the piano by imitating and memorizing the keyboard activity generated by piano rolls. Later, he was formally tutored in the stride idiom, first by Russell Brooks and then, probably beginning in 1921, by the acknowledged master of the style, James P. Johnson.[8] He accompanied silent movies on pipe organ at the Lincoln and Lafayette theaters in Harlem and occasionally played for vaudeville shows as well. In 1922 he began his long and substantial recording career by accompanying blues singers and by cutting twenty-two piano rolls and part of a twenty-third for the QRS Company (mostly in 1923–24).

Waller also played regularly at rent parties in Harlem in the early 1920s (and through the end of the decade as well, though with less frequency).[9] These affairs, organized both as social occasions at which young African Americans could congregate and as opportunities for the host to bolster his or her economic well-being, depended for their success on the ability of pianists to provide hours of almost continuous music for dancing. Stride, with its rhythmic bass and elegantly crafted right hand embellishments, was a style well suited to this task. Indeed, it was the need to supply dance music over long, uninterrupted stretches of time that prompted stride pianists to develop their individual repertoires of complex but endlessly adaptable "tricks."[10] Pianists became identified with such signature gestures and other distinctive musical strategies. Informal (but deeply serious) competitions between well-known pianists, known as cutting contests, could occur spontaneously or might be advertised as the featured event at rent parties. Because such contests required performing at the highest level of virtuosity, athleticism, and endurance, they became part of the defining aesthetic for an aspiring stride pianist, and Waller took full advantage of the opportunities they offered.

---

[5]Waller and Calabrese, *Fats Waller,* 6.

[6]Waller and Calabrese, *Fats Waller,* 6–7.

[7]Kirkeby, *Ain't Misbehavin',* 11.

[8]Johnson recalled that the first time he heard Waller play "he had fervor—he was the son of a preacher, you know—but he didn't have any swing then." After Johnson started giving Waller regular instruction, he [Johnson] would "get on one piano, [Waller would] get on the other, and we'd work together. This went on for a couple of years, steady. He picked up all the stomps and rags I knew and that walkin' bass, too." Seymour Peck, "PM Visits: The Dean of Jazz Pianists," *PM* (Friday, 27 April 1945): 20.

[9]A detailed overview of rent parties and the musical activity they engendered may be found in Scott E. Brown, *James P. Johnson: A Case of Mistaken Identity* (Metuchen, N. J.: The Scarecrow Press and the Institute of Jazz Studies, Rutgers University, 1982), 165–75. See also Paul S. Machlin, *Stride: The Music of Fats Waller* (Boston: Twayne Publishers, 1985), 9–11.

[10]In the context of stride piano music, tricks are brief decorative figures, usually but not exclusively for the right hand; often these gestures are brief enough to be repeated several times over the stride bass pattern as it passes through the harmonic changes of a phrase.

After devoting the first half of the 1920s to his apprenticeship, Waller entered a more intensive period of creative work, focusing on three overlapping areas of musical activity: composing, recording, and performing. Between 1926 and 1929 he composed independent songs for Tin Pan Alley, as well as songs for no fewer than five shows and revues: *Tan Town Topics, Junior Blackbirds, Keep Shufflin', Load of Coal,* and *Hot Chocolates.*[11] At the same time, he had begun to record for the Victor Company on a regular basis. From 1927 to 1929 he produced a catalog of recordings that demonstrated his mastery of stride on both piano and pipe organ. Moreover, at many of these sessions he made alternate takes—two or more performances of a particular song recorded consecutively at the same session. Such concentrated work on selected repertoire honed his technical skill at the keyboard and encouraged him to vary his interpretations. Limited studio time and the permanence of sound recording may well have inspired Waller to a new level of proficiency. As the magnitude and quality of his later output indicates, these years in the studio prepared him to be focused and efficient during recording sessions without becoming repetitive. Ultimately, Waller achieved a level of skill that made alternate takes all but superfluous, and they rarely appear in the logs of recording sessions held during the later years of his career.[12] Finally, the number of his live performances steadily increased, taking place in shows and nightclubs and before a wider and more diverse, but no less appreciative, audience than he had entertained at private rent parties.[13]

Waller's increased recording activity in the late 1920s was prompted by the dramatic rise of the recording industry itself. His position as an entertainer was enhanced further by the enthusiasm in American life and culture for radio—a technology firmly entrenched by the end of the decade. It was principally these media, individually and in combination, that introduced Waller's work to a broad, multiracial public. By a coincidence crucial to the growth of his reputation, he achieved a new level of artistic maturity just as the operations of the two media began to converge, creating new avenues of commercial opportunity for performers of popular music (and enriching their producers as well).

By 1930 radio had become the herald of American popular culture, and Waller performed regularly over the airwaves for about six months in 1931 in New York, and from late 1932 to early 1934 in Cincinnati.[14] His success with radio's audience derived from the brilliance of his playing, as well as from the sassy textual variants and exaggerated delivery of the lyrics he incorporated into his singing. Waller capitalized on these devices, developing a rapport with his listeners that did not depend on visual contact to promote a sense of intimacy. While there are no known airchecks of Waller's radio performances from the early 1930s, the essence of his vocal style is apparent on the first extant example of his singing on a solo recording, "I'm Crazy 'Bout My Baby" (Transcription 5a, 13 March 1931, mx. 151417-3). Although he had recorded this same song one week earlier with Ted Lewis and His Band (6 March 1931, mx. 151396-1), it is the later recording that reveals for the first time the full range of his wit.[15]

---

[11]According to a chronological list of Waller's songs compiled by Howard Rye, eighty-three titles were copyrighted in Waller's name between 1926 and 1929. See Laurie Wright, *"Fats" in Fact* (Chigwell, Essex: Storyville Publications, 1992), 444–52.

[12]See Machlin, *Stride,* 78–79.

[13]Waller composed for and appeared in *Keep Shufflin',* which opened in New York on 27 February 1928; he played piano for the premiere of James P. Johnson's rhapsody *Yamekraw* at Carnegie Hall on 27 April 1928; and he composed and played for two shows in 1929 at the nightclub Connie's Inn—*Load of Coal* and *Hot Chocolates.*

[14]See Kirkeby, *Ain't Misbehavin',* 144, 160–64 and Alyn Shipton, *Fats Waller, His Life and Times* (Tunbridge Wells: Spellmount, 1988), 56. The exact dates of Waller's broadcasts apparently cannot be determined.

[15]See Machlin, *Stride,* 33–37.

Waller entered into an exclusive recording contract with Victor in 1934, and from mid-May of that year until shortly before August 1942, when the American Federation of Musicians' recording ban went into effect, he was both disciplined and prolific in the studio. Meanwhile, he continued to maintain a hectic and ultimately debilitating schedule of club dates, went on domestic and foreign tours (Europe in 1938 and 1939), and appeared in two short Hollywood films in 1935 (*Hooray for Love!* and *King of Burlesque*).[16] In 1941 he made so-called "soundies" of four of his most popular songs: "Honeysuckle Rose," "Ain't Misbehavin'," "Your Feet's Too Big," and "The Joint Is Jumpin'."[17] In his final appearance on film, *Stormy Weather* (1943), he took on a minor comic role and played the part with obvious relish.[18]

Despite his heavy performing and recording schedule, Waller—always a fluent and rapid songwriter—found time to compose. But after 1934 his annual output of published compositions decreased, occasionally dwindling to only a few titles. By this time, though, Waller was a seasoned craftsman. His published music reflected both familiarity with Tin Pan Alley's verse and chorus structures and the ability to conceive an appealing melodic line to convey the essence of the lyric. Waller also mastered the use of tonal harmony to support a melody that was sensitive to the inflection and rhythmic patterns of the text. A study of his published music alone, however, cannot fully explain Waller's approach to composition in the idiom of popular song. A more complete account of his compositional activity emerges when his songs are considered within the legacy of his performances.

Waller's Compositional Process

Waller's skills as a performer deeply influenced his compositional process. At the core of his musical rhetoric lies a total command of stride technique. In a 1936 interview in which he prescribed an essential curriculum for the aspiring stride player, he summarized the basic elements of that technique, as he himself must have learned them:

> It's all in knowing what to put on the right beat. . . . First get a thorough bass. Make it more rhythmic than flashy, a pulsating bass. Know how to play first without pedals and then always use the pedals sparingly. Study harmony so you will know the chords. Play clean both in the right and left hand. This is one of the marks of the modern pianist, he plays much cleaner than the old school. There is also much more expression to modern playing and it is necessary to know how to build climaxes, how to raise up and let down, to show sudden contracts [*sic;* probably *contrasts*]. Keep the right hand always subservient to the melody. Trying to do too much always detracts from the tune.[19]

Waller's criteria for excellence, then, rest on fundamental musical principles involving rhythm, pedaling, harmony, accuracy in execution, dramatic expression, and unobtru-

---

[16]Duke Ellington also appeared in a film in 1935, *Symphony in Black,* for which he wrote the score (which, given its programmatic intent, was presumably developed in close conjunction with the film's scenario). Though contemporaries, Waller and Ellington promoted diametrically opposed views of African-American jazz musicians in their film appearances: Waller as lighthearted musician/comedian and Ellington as earnest composer/performer. Ellington's seriousness of purpose in *Symphony in Black* is underscored not only by the film's outline of racial history that the music is intended to illustrate, but also by the visual formality of the concert hall staging in which Ellington and the orchestra appear. (Among other details, Ellington conducts the orchestra from an open grand piano in white tie and tails.) The two musicians nevertheless remained staunch admirers of each other's work; for them the distinction between comic and serious was not one of depth or integrity.

[17]These were brief film clips of performances of single songs, about three and one-half minutes long and viewed through public juke-box projectors.

[18]Waller's appearances on film are discussed in detail in Shipton, *Fats Waller,* 75–86.

[19]Quoted in *Metronome* 52:2 (February 1936): 33. The interviewer is not identified; Waller's comments were probably edited for publication.

sive embellishment. His recordings reflect the value he placed on such musical parameters in performance, as the transcriptions in this volume reveal. But although the gestures that result from his application of these principles may appear spontaneous in performance, they derive from skills he refined through years of practice and experience. Indeed, the case can be made that Waller uses his performance skills in a compositional, perhaps even premeditated, way.

In the 1936 interview, Waller first cites two aspects of rhythm in stride—what to put on the right beat and how to achieve a rhythmic, pulsating bass. Perhaps by focusing first on rhythm, he intends to emphasize its importance. Certainly rhythm is a crucial element in his own playing; his performances almost always project a sense of drive, propulsion, and momentum. He achieves this effect in part through anticipation and accent in the left hand, often sounding the bottom pitch of a downbeat chord just before the beat and accenting the upper pitches of the chord on the downbeat. He occasionally varies this basic pattern of attack, substituting either a chord or single pitch on the downbeat, or sounding four equally accented chords in the left hand on each beat of the measure. (Each of these patterns occurs in Transcription 3a, "Waiting At The End of The Road," 29 August 1929, mx. 55375-2; see mm. 28–36.) Yet these patterns can be subject to even further refinement. For example, instead of four accented chords, Waller might play the top pitch of each quarter-note chord before the beat, as he does for downbeat chords, except that they are rolled downward in pitch instead of upward (see Transcription 5a, "I'm Crazy 'Bout My Baby," 13 March 1931, mx. 151417-3, mm. 61–62). Finally, Waller's right hand will usually enhance the swing created by the left, often by syncopating the melody (see Transcription 1b, "Gladyse," 2 August 1929, mx. 49496-2, mm. 116–18). However, this cooperative relationship between the hands could be undercut. Occasionally, his right hand melodies and passagework bear little or no relation to the forward momentum of the left hand, as if they were floating independently above the bass. In performance this effect is produced by subtly anticipating or delaying a pitch or gesture, or by stretching or accelerating a particular passage (see Transcription 8b, "I Ain't Got Nobody," 11 June 1937, mx. 010656-1, mm. 64–68; and also Transcription 6b, "Honeysuckle Rose, à la Bach, Beethoven, Brahms, and Waller," 13 May 1941, mx. 063890-1, mm. 83–87). In such instances, the right hand's relation to the left is analogous to a singer's relation to the accompaniment. Waller's own singing often demonstrates a similar flexibility (see Transcription 4b, "I Can't Give You Anything But Love," 3 November 1939, mx. 043351-2, mm. 43–55).

Waller's injunction to "know the chords" is another criterion for playing stride that carries important implications for his composing. A comparison of alternate takes is instructive in this regard. The introductions he devises for the two takes of "I Can't Give You Anything But Love" recorded on 3 November 1939 (Transcriptions 4a/b), for example, are startlingly different, particularly in their harmonic substructure. The opening measures of the first take vacillate amiably between tonic and dominant, while in the second take the analogous passage begins with a striking dissonance on the relative minor and meanders chromatically through a series of descending parallel tenth chords until arriving at the dominant. Whether these two openings were preconceived or improvised, it is clear that only a pianist who "knows the chords" could offer such contrasting, yet organic and equally effective, introductions.

A third element is the stipulation to "keep the right hand always subservient to the melody." Adding that "Trying to do too much always detracts from the tune," Waller seems to be suggesting that the application of (mostly) right-hand tricks—the process of embellishing the melody in stride—must be accomplished with finesse and restraint. And indeed, despite the complexity of some of Waller's ornamentation, the essence of the tune in his performances is never overshadowed or muddied by decoration. Here it is the injunction itself, rather than its application in performance, that reveals a composer's bias—an impulse to preserve in recognizable form the melody as originally conceived.

Structure, an essential element of composition, does not appear in Waller's list. Yet he subjects even this most basic component of a song's identity to variation in performance. Much like many composers of written song, Waller tinkers in performance with the length and number of choruses, as well as the length and purpose of opening, transitional, and concluding passages—as if trying to find the most effective overall shape to express his musical intent. Again, such variation in form occurs even from one take to the next in the same session (see Transcriptions 2a/b, "Rusty Pail Blues," 14 January 1927, mxx. 37362-1/37362-3).

Waller's creative activity as a composer of popular song reveals his adherence to the same fundamental principles that guided his choices as a performer. The several notated sketches for his music that have survived provide another window into the compositional process. The challenge in assessing this notated work is twofold. The central task is to locate and examine the available evidence documenting the genesis of his compositions—that is, to conduct sketch studies that build on established procedures within the discipline of musicology. But to take that step, it is first necessary to dispel a persistent myth about Waller's work habits as a composer.

Jazz musicians in performance tend to adopt a public persona cultivated from elements of their character. In Waller's case, the essence of this persona was exuberance, which he projected clearly and forcefully. ("Exuberance," he once remarked, "is the spontaneity of life."[20]) This characterization rests in part on fact: certainly in public, and by all accounts in most aspects of his private life as well, he manifested a lively, extroverted, and generous spirit. However, his reputation for buoyancy also stems from the seemingly apocryphal stories told by the musicians he worked with, as well as by some of his biographers. Where composition is concerned, these stories tend to couple a gift for quick inspiration with an off-the-cuff attitude towards the routine of composing, especially the sketching, drafting, and revising that creative work in any written genre requires.[21] Anecdotes in this vein have become such an enduring part of his biography, and indeed of the conventional wisdom about jazz, that they overshadow the idea of Waller as a working composer.[22] But just as Waller's influence as a performer may be traced through careful evaluation of the enormous body of recorded work he produced, so a more balanced and nuanced account of his compositional activity emerges from the evidence documenting those very real labors. Far from being cavalier about his written work, Waller was a disciplined and methodical craftsman, as shown by his contributions to the 1943 Broadway musical *Early to Bed*—his last major compositional effort.

Waller's work on *Early to Bed* is illuminated by recordings and documents surviving from the early stages of the production. Two collections (the Victor Amerling Collection of musical sketch material and the Clifford Morris Collection of recordings—see Sources) contain materials that afford an unusually comprehensive picture of Waller's work on this one project. The musical notation preserved by Amerling's documents

---

[20]Waller makes this comment as an aside in his 12 January 1940 recording of "Mighty Fine" (mx. 044602-1).

[21]Kirkeby's version of Waller's composition of "My Fate Is In Your Hands" is typical: " 'Perfect!' said Fats, chewing on a fried chicken bone. 'How's this?' He played a scrap of melody . . . Fats repeated the phrase, then played it over again, then added another phrase. In another minute he had completed eight bars. In an hour he had the ballad completed" (Kirkeby, *Ain't Misbehavin'*, 122). Mary Lou Williams offers another such anecdote: "Mary Lou recalled Waller sitting 'overflowing the piano stool' with his jug of whisky nearby. [Leonard] Harper [the choreographer who worked with Waller at Connie's Inn] called out to ask what Fats had written for the next routine, and—according to Mary Lou—Fats made up the show there and then, improvising something appropriate for each routine" (Shipton, *Fats Waller*, 41).

[22]"Some of his songs were dashed off in taxis *en route* to recording sessions, others simply improvised at the piano in the studio with apparent spontaneity" (Bruce Crowther and Mike Pinfold, *Singing Jazz: The Singers and their Styles* [London: Blandford, 1997], 67).

allows us to trace the evolution of individual songs, chart the progress of Waller's creative efforts with some degree of precision, and make reasonable hypotheses about the musical criteria that guided his choices. Some of the documents contain clearly preliminary material, yet they bear no trace of revision, as might be expected in a sketch. With Waller, that appears to reflect not a lack of interest in the project, but rather the ease with which ideas came to him and the rapid pace at which he worked. Other documents, specifically drafts of several of the songs, contain many revisions and occasionally reveal Waller's struggle to decide among various alternatives; this kind of intensive labor verifies his commitment to the quality of his compositional work for the show. The recordings yield at least one intact version for many of the show's songs as played by the composer. These discs were probably made by Waller as demonstration takes for the show's producer and writer, and they disclose fresh, often intriguing interpretations of the newly composed material, and hint at the interaction between writing and playing in Waller's compositional approach.

Richard Kollmar, the producer of *Early to Bed* (also the director and male lead), hired Waller early in 1943 to appear as a performer in the cast of the show.[23] Following their return to New York, after filming *Stormy Weather* in Hollywood in January and early February 1943, Waller and his manager entered into detailed negotiations with Kollmar. Kollmar apparently revealed that he had not yet chosen a composer for the show, and Kirkeby convinced him, partly on the basis of Waller's record as a composer of scores for musicals, to hire Waller. George Marion Jr., the lyricist, agreed to the collaboration. Waller thus became the only African American in the show's creative hierarchy, and *Early to Bed,* one of the very few Broadway shows for white audiences for which an African American was engaged as principal composer.[24] *Early to Bed* opened in Boston for its tryout run for two weeks on 24 May 1943 and premiered in New York at the Broadhurst Theater on 17 June 1943.[25] It ran for 382 performances, well into 1944. Waller's untimely death, just six months after the opening, apparently deeply affected Kollmar, who delivered a heartfelt tribute to the composer at his funeral service.[26]

Early to Bed's book was condemned by the New York critics as unusually lackluster. Lewis Nichols's review in *The New York Times* is typical: "*Early to Bed,* which opened last evening at the Broadhurst, is long on body and short on mind. It undoubtedly has the most beautiful chorus in the land, and its costumes and designs definitely are prepriority, but it also has one of the most tedious books on record."[27] Waller's music, however, was widely praised. Even a German language newspaper, the *New Yorker Staats-Zeitung,* expressed delight in the music, once its critic got around to mentioning it: "O ja, fast hätten wir die Musik vergessen. Die ist von Fats Waller, sehr prägnant, sehr witzig, und in einigen Fällen, einprägsam . . . Sie ist auch spritzig und schwungsvoll."[28] ("Oh yes, we almost forgot about the music. It's by Fats Waller, very tight, very clever, and in some cases, catchy . . . It is also effervescent and snappy.")

There were fourteen songs in the Boston tryout version; one of these was dropped for the New York run. Sketches and drafts may be found for twelve of the remaining thirteen, and for many other songs apparently intended for the show but never used. A

---

23 Kirkeby, *Ain't Misbehavin',* 218–19.

24 Only one other Broadway show of this period seems to have been constructed by a similarly racially diverse team: *Policy Kings* of 1939, for which James P. Johnson was the composer and Louis Douglass the lyricist; see Brown, *James P. Johnson,* 273.

25 Other Broadway shows playing at this time, the height of World War II, included Thornton Wilder's *The Skin of Our Teeth,* Maxwell Anderson's *The Eve of St. Mark, Oklahoma, The Student Prince,* and an edition of *Ziegfeld Follies* with Milton Berle. See inter alia, Gerald Bordman, *American Musical Theater, A Chronicle* (New York: Oxford University Press, 1978), 534–37.

26 Waller and Calabrese, *Fats Waller,* 179.

27 Lewis Nichols, "The Play In Review: 'Early to Bed,'" *The New York Times,* 18 June 1943.

28 *New Yorker Staats-Zeitung,* 21 June 1943.

draft for one of the abandoned songs, "One–Two," will illuminate a few general traits of these working documents (see plate 1, "3rd One–Two"). Waller used pencil to write out this version of the melody,[29] which may be categorized as a draft rather than a sketch since it is a clean, unedited copy of this version of the tune. Because the document bears the designation "3rd" as well as the song's title, this draft probably represents Waller's third attempt to set these lyrics to music. And in fact, the collection contains two additional drafts for the song, each with a melody fundamentally different from the one in this draft. The date written at the top of "3rd One–Two" is "Sunday, Mar. 7," [1943].[30]

The draft of "One–Two" typifies Waller's working documents in other ways. First, pairs of staves are linked together to form braces; this is one of two standard manuscript configurations Waller used, even when sketching a melodic line without accompaniment. (The other consists of a single staff line.) Second, Waller draws clef signs and key signatures only on the first brace. The indications typical of Waller's hand in these symbols include the curvature of the treble clef, the shape of the common time signature, and the strongly slanted lines of the sharp signs. In fact, Waller usually gives all his horizontal lines a similar slant, as may be noted in the uppercase letters "E" and "T" of the title words. The distinctive "V" shape of the quarter rests is also characteristic. Finally, Waller includes a few cursory chord indications for the first musical phrase.[31]

Two documents for another song from *Early To Bed* contain almost identical music, yet they bear somewhat different titles (see plate 2, "Horse in Blue," and plate 3, "Wonderful/Horse in Blue"). The sketch for "Horse in Blue" has been prepared in a manner similar to the "One–Two" draft, in that individual staves are linked by pairs to form braces, and clef signs and key signatures are drawn only at the beginning of the document and of sections. (In the "Horse In Blue" sketch, clef and key signs appear at the introduction, at the chorus, and again at the beginning of the verse.) The shape and general appearance of the quarter notes suggest that Waller sketched this tune rapidly, completing the chorus and the first eight-measure phrase of the verse. At that point, however, he must have gone back over the sketch to reshape the rhythmic profile of one gesture in the chorus, that of measures 3, 7, 19, and 23 (as counted from the beginning of the chorus; see example 1; note how the eighth notes and eighth rests have become quarters and the half note has been filled to form a quarter). Waller usually wrote with a particular text in mind, and his melodic lines were always sensitive to the inflection and rhythmic cadence of the lyric. The basic rhythm of the figure in example 1 seems derived from the natural pattern of accents in the song's title, "Horse in Blue," when spoken. Of Waller's two alternatives for these words, however, the revised profile (example 1b) gives greater punch to the downbeat (made explicit by Waller's addition of an accent mark) and sets up the syncopated final beat of the measure, consistent with emphasizing the two important words of the title.

A dub of Waller's homemade acetate recording of this song survives in the Clifford Morris Collection.[32] Not surprisingly the sound quality is poor with a persistent echo throughout the cut. In addition, the recording speed is not quite true, and as a result

[29]The manuscript paper for almost all these documents is twelve-stave OPQ brand.

[30]Though the year is not specified, March 7 occurred on a Sunday during Waller's later years only in 1937, when he was not engaged in any major projects like composing the score for a show, and in 1943, the year *Early to Bed* was written and produced. Thus, the document helps narrow the timing for Waller's work on *Early to Bed* to March 1943.

[31]Though this document may be classified as a draft (i.e., a finished copy), it nevertheless appears as though Waller made some revisions. He altered the rhythmic profile of measures 3 and 11 by superimposing a half note over the original quarter note. In addition, there is an unresolved rhythmic ambiguity in measures 9, 13, and 25, each of which contains five beats instead of four, perhaps the result of haste.

[32]Kirkeby has inaccurately titled the dub "Horse Blues" in his typewritten index to the reels of tape; see note 34.

Example 1. Adjustments to rhythmic profile in sketch for "Horse in Blue" (plate 2)

a. original

the performance sounds a half step lower than the written pitch of the sketch. The recording's value lies not in its fidelity, however, but in what it discloses of Waller's playing style. Ever the improviser, Waller extends the introduction beyond what appears in the sketch and also substitutes new material in his first statement of the chorus at measures 25–28 (see example 2). This first statement has a rhapsodic quality, produced by the rhythmic freedom in Waller's playing; by contrast, the second statement of the chorus, propelled by the stately swing in Waller's left hand, is metrically regular.[33] Finally, for all its technical shortcomings, the recording preserves Waller's intensity of expression in performance, conveyed through delicate phrasing and extremes of dynamic range.

The second of the two documents containing music for this song was probably intended as a fair copy of the same melody, drafted on a single staff (see plate 3, "Wonderful/Horse in Blue"). Originally, this may have been a reasonably neat copy, incorporating the new rhythmic profile Waller had engineered for measures 3, 7, 19, and 23. But it also shows a number of substantial revisions: Waller scratched out the old working title and replaced it with the new title's catchword ("Wonderful," as in "You're Only Slightly Less Than Wonderful").[34] He also recast measures 15–16, replacing the oscillating gesture of the "Horse in Blue" sketch with a rising line that conforms to the original rhythm (see example 3). However, he also placed a symbol (an X within a circle) above each of these two measures. This symbol appears like an asterisk at the bottom of the page, above a sketch that reproduces the original form of the same two

Example 2. Comparison of sketched and recorded versions of "Horse in Blue"

a. sketched

b. recorded

[33]Later in his career, Waller occasionally makes a similar distinction between first and second choruses of piano solos by contrasting rhapsodic and regular tempos. "Hallelujah," recorded 7 August 1939 (Muzak Associated disc number ZZ 2146), provides an extreme example of this contrast; "Tea for Two," recorded at the same session (Muzak Associated disc number ZZ 2145), offers a somewhat less dramatic contrast between the opening verse and the first chorus.

[34]"Horse in Blue" is probably a ghost title, that is, a nonsense phrase devised to mirror the inflection and rhythmic accent of the actual title's catchword—"Wonderful." It is this ghost title that could have led Kirkeby to rename the recording yet again, but inaccurately, as "Horse Blues"—he may have thought the tune was actually a blues and that Waller's use of the preposition "in" was therefore mistaken.

measures. Waller may have contemplated restoring this gesture from the "Horse in Blue" sketch, but he evidently reconsidered, scratching out the original at the bottom of the page and confirming his preference for the new version by writing the word "good" under the revised measures.

Waller lavished considerable care on the last four measures of the chorus. After erasing the original form of the line (barely visible in plate 3, but transcribed as example 4a), he completed no fewer than four alternatives before settling on one of them—indicating his preference here as well by noting "good" in the margin (see examples 4b–e). Perhaps an examination of these variant endings in the order in which they were composed would reveal how Waller refined his material until he achieved the final version. But another, more likely, explanation for the multiple versions of this passage lies in Waller's experience as a stride pianist. Playing stride requires a pianist to maintain a substantial vocabulary of decorative musical gestures that can be used to embellish melodic lines. Indeed, applying such gestures to preexisting material forms a major component of stride improvisation. In this light, any one of Waller's options may serve as an ending for the phrase; for Waller, it would simply be a matter of choosing among alternatives in the course of performance. In fact, when he made a V-Disc recording[35] of this song at the Victor studios on 16 September 1943,[36] Waller added yet another alternative to the ones appearing in this document (see example 4f), closing the chorus by combining the first two bars of example 4e with the last two of example 4d.

Irrepressible and consummate entertainer that he was, Waller introduces the V-Disc recording, intended for broadcast to soldiers, with a bit of comedy. He also inserts a plug for *Early to Bed,* for there was always the chance that some listeners might later become paying customers for the show: "Now boys, I'm gonna give you a couple of tunes from my show *Early to Bed,* a fine show on Broadway that, uh, pays my cathouse dues, you know?" After a chorus for piano solo, Waller launches into a vocal chorus, but his text differs from the one filed on the copyright card in the Library of Congress and credited to George Marion, Jr., the show's lyricist. Waller's recorded lyric is possibly a second, unpublished verse by Marion or perhaps one written by Waller or his longtime collaborator Andy Razaf (see example 5).[37] Waller seems to have had little inclination to provide a straight rendition of almost any lyric, and he freely embellishes even this V-Disc variant. For example, he applies an extended rolled "r" to the words "wrap" and "around," at once evoking and mocking the presumed snobbery of those

Example 3. Melodic changes to sketch of "Wonderful/Horse in Blue" (plate 3)

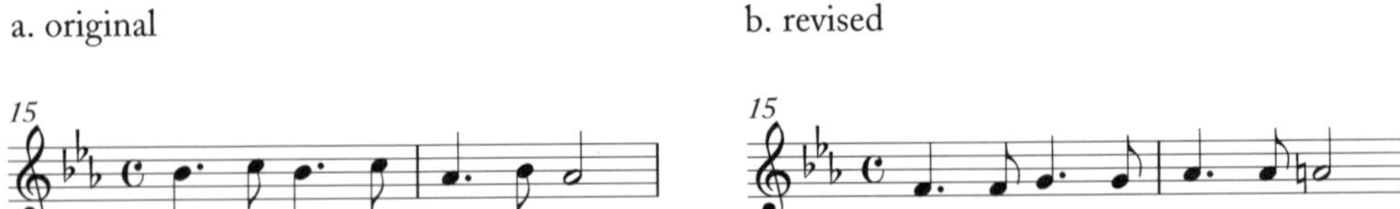

[35]V-Discs were sound recordings produced in New York City during and after World War II by the Armed Forces. They provided entertainment for service personnel on active duty abroad; by agreement with the American Federation of Musicians, the Music Publishers' Protective Association, and the American Federation of Radio Artists, they were not made available commercially.

[36]Waller was invited to record the V-Disc by Steve Sholes; this was his first session at the Victor studios since July 1942, due to the musicians' union recording ban, which had gone into effect in August 1942. At this session, very nearly Waller's last, he recorded five songs from *Early to Bed:* "You're Only Slightly Less Than Wonderful," "There's a Gal in My Life," "This Is So Nice It Must Be Illegal," "(There's Yes in the Air in) Martinique," and "The Ladies Who Sing with the Band."

[37]Waller may have felt that the new, racier lyric would be more entertaining than the original for an audience of soldiers.

Example 4. Variants for closing measures of chorus for "Wonderful/Horse in Blue"

Example 5. Transcription of varied lyric from Waller's V-Disc performance of "Wonderful," recorded 16 September 1943

> You're only slightly less than wonderful,
> Your body borders on the murderous,
> I think I'm on the brink of buying you mink,
> To drag on the ground, or wrap around you when you slink;
> Within me elemental forces surge,
> Are you allergic to the orgy urge?
> Must I with deep regret let etiquette guide me as yet—
> And say to you politely, dear, you're only slightly less than wonderful.

who could afford to purchase mink. When he imposes a simpering inflection on this already affected pronunciation, an even more stinging satire results.

Another set of sketches and drafts contain music for a song titled "That Does It." This song was originally intended for *Early to Bed,* but was eventually dropped. The document establishing this provenance includes a list of six song titles in Waller's hand, among them "That Does It" (see plate 4, "Long Time No Song"), as well as fragments of music for "Long Time No Song," "Early to Bed," and "Jump No. 1."[38] Waller numbered the list of titles consecutively with Roman numerals. Only two of the songs on the list, "At the Hi-De Oh [*sic:* Ho] High in Harlem" and "Early to Bed," appear in the Boston and New York programs for the show. However, the way Waller has grouped the titles together in a list suggests that at some stage of the show's development, he imagined using all six of them.

One version of "That Does It," probably Waller's first attempt, was sketched on paper that had been prepared for the song "When the Nylons Bloom Again" (see plate 5, "That Does It/Nylons Bloom"). Waller apparently required only two corrections in this sketch. First, he revised the rhythm of the descending line in measures 9 and 11. In its original form, the figure's total duration of three beats came up one beat short in a four-beat measure, so Waller rectified this deficiency by changing the final quarter note to a half note. Second, in measures 13–15, he altered the rhythmic profile of the ascending leap from two eighth notes to two half notes, writing "good" below the change to confirm his preference.[39] In addition to these two alterations, the sketch bears more evidence of haste. In measure 34, almost the last measure of the chorus, Waller outlined a figure whose rhythm suggests that it was intended for the title words—"that does it." But the figure's placement within the measure creates a syncopated pattern for the title phrase that does not fit the natural accentuation of those words. It is unlikely that Waller would have overlooked this awkwardness at a later stage in drafting the song, and indeed, in all other versions of the song except one, this gesture has been revised.

A second document (see plate 6, "2n") provides a more polished version of the song. The designation "2n" (presumably denoting "second") at the top of the sheet suggests that it may have been written out after the melody sketch, but it may still not represent Waller's final version. (His performance on the acetate recording, for example, follows the melody sketch more closely, in some respects, than the "2n" sketch.) Whatever the sequence of these two documents, Waller wrote out the harmonic underpinning of the melody in the "2n" draft, perhaps adding parts of this accompaniment after first writing out the melody in full. (Note, for example, the addition of a lower voice in the right-hand octaves of the opening gesture, and in similar places throughout the draft.) This document departs from the melody sketch in three other ways. Waller altered slightly the rhythmic pattern of measures 9, 11, 25, and 27 (see examples 6a–b), he revised the close of the first sixteen-measure section (mm. 13–15; see example 7), and he adjusted the rhythmic placement of the final gesture (mm. 33–36; see example 8).

A third document contains a draft of the melody of "That Does It," paired with a draft of "Long Time." Both are clean, unedited copies—fair copies or final drafts—suggesting that they contain final versions of each song.[40] "Long Time" was eventually included in the version of the show that played in New York, but "That Does It" was not (though this pairing, like the document in plate 4, offers evidence that the number

38 The distinctive slant to Waller's horizontal lines on uppercase letters such as "T," "H," and "E," as well as similar lines at the top and bottom of the Roman numerals, establish this as a list that Waller himself wrote out.

39 It is clear that the half-note configuration was sketched after the eighth notes; all other half notes have been drawn with their stems up, not down, as in the redrawn notes. Another justification for this conclusion may be found in other measures of the sketch that originally contained just two half notes (mm. 1–2, 5–6, etc.); there, Waller has drawn the second half note relatively close to the bar line. From the spacing of those unretouched measures, then, one can infer that if Waller had drawn two half notes originally in measures 13–15, he would not have left enough space between the second half note and the bar line to accommodate two quarter rests. But because in measures 13–15 he pencils in the half notes over his original configuration (two eighth notes/one quarter note/two quarter rests), the second of the two half notes appears approximately in the center of the measure (adjacent to the quarter note it is to replace) instead of where it might otherwise be expected it to appear, i.e., closer to the bar line.

40 Both drafts are consistent in format with the draft of "Wonderful/Horse In Blue" (plate 3).

Example 6. "That Does It," rhythmic patterns in mm. 9, 11, 25, 27, plus variants in Transcription 9

a. melody sketch (plate 5)

b. "2n" sketch (plate 6)

c. first variant, m. 17

d. second variant, mm. 35 and 55

e. third variant, m. 53

Example 7. "That Does It," measures 13–15

a. melody sketch (plate 5)

b. "2n" sketch (plate 6)

Example 8. "That Does It," closing gesture, mm. 33–36

a. melody sketch (plate 5)

b. "2n" sketch (plate 6)

was certainly intended for *Early to Bed*). Indeed, the juxtaposition of these two drafts in this third document suggests further that "That Does It" may well have been prepared in rehearsal and perhaps even kept in the show until shortly before the tryout. In any event, the music in this third draft preserves the form of the tune found in the first sketch of the melody (plate 5).

Waller's acetate recording of "That Does It"[41] (Transcription 9) follows the melody sketch of the music as noted above, but with two exceptions. For the gesture of measures 11 and 25 from the sketch (now mm. 19 and 33 in the transcription because of the added eight-bar introduction), Waller used the revised rhythmic configuration of the "2n" version of the melody (see example 6b). In the parallel places to measures 9 and 27 (mm. 17 and 35 in the transcription), Waller introduces yet more rhythmic variety, playing 6c and d, respectively. Yet another rhythmic displacement of this figure (6e) appears in measure 53 of the second chorus, suggesting that this tactic of continual rhythmic variation is one of Waller's improvisational strategies. Waller's other significant departure from the sketch is found in the closing passage of the second chorus. Here he ignored both sketches. Instead of articulating again the parallel ninth chords in quarter notes that appear in the "2n" sketch in measures 29–33 (plate 6), as might be expected at the close of the second chorus, Waller broadened the harmonic progression over several measures, moving through what is basically an enriched II–V–I^{6}–vi pattern (the analogous passage begins in m. 72 of the transcription). He then replaced the definitive cadential figures used as a conclusion in all three documents—the melody sketch, the harmonized draft ("2n"), and the fair copy of the melody—with the passage beginning at measure 79. This new ending surprises in three respects: it eliminates the final upward flourish that closes the written melody, it is restricted to the lower register of the piano, and its rhythmic profile consists exclusively of quarter notes.

The delicacy of touch in Waller's playing that emanates from the closing twelve measures of this recording, coupled with the slower harmonic pace and the syncopated, chromatically descending bass line, provides a marked contrast to the energy implied in the written ending. This understated quality surfaces in Waller's performances in the 1940s with a frequency that might at first appear exceptional for one whose playing is so often described as energetic and ebullient. Yet, on return from his 1938 European tour Waller reportedly said, "For years I've been trying to sell the idea of softer stuff over here. I used to tell 'em down at Victor I ought to tone down, but they'd just say, 'No, go ahead and give 'em that hot primitive stuff.' "[42]

Whether Waller may have wanted to explore a greater range of expression in his playing or to pursue some other artistic urge is difficult to gauge. (Maurice Waller suggests that by the end of the 1930s his father had begun to take his potential as a composer more seriously: "He constantly talked about his admiration for Gershwin's *Rhapsody in Blue* and *Concerto in F.* He was introducing more and more classical themes into his music."[43]) Perhaps this less extroverted style constitutes simply a considered response to the commercially successful persona he had come to adopt as a performer. Wherever the truth lies among the range of possibilities, the evidence at hand contradicts the notion that Waller took the challenge of composing lightly. Exuberance and spontaneity aside, the pianist was also a professional craftsman whose calling required a thorough command of particular musical techniques. These two closely related collections (the Victor Amerling Collection of sketches and the Clifford Morris Collection of recordings) reveal both Waller's depth as a performer and his developing strength as a composer—a strength that was tested for what was to prove the final time in his work on the score for *Early to Bed.*

---

[41]At the beginning of this recording one can detect the machine winding itself up to speed, though as in the acetate recording of the misnamed tune "Horse Blues" (i.e., "You're Only Slightly Less Than Wonderful") the performance sounds a half step lower than the key of the sketch.

[42]"Fats Waller 'Learns' From European Bands," *New York World Telegram,* 12 November 1938: 10.

[43]Waller and Calabrese, *Fats Waller,* 136; see also Introduction: *Parody.*

"You Got Me Walkin', Talkin', and Squawkin'": What Waller Signifies

Waller has been widely appreciated for his engaging wit and humor. That he was very funny is generally taken for granted, but some critics have dismissed his richly textured comedy as simple buffoonery, failing to acknowledge the way it comments on and critiques the traditions from which it stems.[44] (The French writer Hughes Panassié, who met Waller during the composer's first sojourn to Paris in 1932, is the notable exception to this critical reception of Waller's work. He perceived the elements of critique latent in Waller's work as early as 1946.[45]) For Waller, however, the use of humor to dramatize or satirize is fundamental to his art; transcription, of course, can only partially reveal this dimension of his artistry.

Waller's humor is perhaps best understood as "signifying," a form of African-American rhetoric characterized by critique and ironic reversal. As Henry Louis Gates, Jr. has written, "Signifyin(g) is black double-voicedness; because it always entails formal revision and an intertextual relation. . . . I find it an ideal metaphor for black literary criticism, or the formal manner in which texts seem concerned to address their antecedents. Repetition with a signal difference is fundamental to the nature of Signifyin(g)."[46] In Gates's analysis, modes of signifying generally exploit the cultural divide between black and white worlds by using African-American expressive resources to transform, recontextualize, or critique language and songs through humor and burlesque. Waller employs at least three basic forms of signifying in his performances, each revealing a sharp intellect at play. First, he satirizes (that is, mocks) aspects of song texts by amending them, changing the words and modifying his delivery of the lines. Second, he engages in antagonistic tactics (put-downs, ranking, and "dissing") towards the audience, the subject of the song, other members of his ensemble, or even himself. And third, he uses his superb piano technique and vast repertoire of pianistic gestures to parody (that is, to imitate in both complimentary and disparaging fashion) particular keyboard styles.[47] Each of these three performative activities contributes to the richness of Waller's signifying.

---

[44]"Whenever possible, Waller jeered and joshed his way into a bumptious burlesque of popular music, but too often the laughs were empty and the enthusiasm forced" (Richard Hadlock, *Jazz Masters of the Twenties* [New York: Macmillan Publishing Co., 1965], 166). "The effect of Waller's vocal mugging is immediate, winning, complete—and it all sounds easy. It *was* easy, I think, and, for most of the musical aspects of Waller's talent, it was also limiting. . . . [A] complex and musically gifted man like Waller might have done a lot more" (Martin Williams, *Jazz Heritage* [Oxford: Oxford University Press, 1985], 15). "Don't bother to ask if Waller had never played the piano could he still entertain us? Rather, even if Waller had never created a note of music he'd still be remembered as one of the great clowns of his epoch. 'Oh, mercy! Sweet apples and pink buttermilk!' " (Will Friedwald, *Jazz Singing* [New York: Charles Scribner's Sons, Macmillan Publishing Company, 1990], 353).

[45]Kirkeby, *Ain't Misbehavin'*, 157. Kirkeby quotes extensively from Panassié's account of Waller's visit to Paris that appeared, according to Kirkeby, in the *PL Yearbook of Jazz, 1946:* "How can [those] who moan . . . at the inanity of American songs, not . . . admire Fats who, well aware of that inanity, but obliged to perform these pieces, turns them completely into ridicule by his remarks, or by the emphatic or farcical manner in which he declaims them."

[46]Henry Louis Gates, Jr., *The Signifying Monkey: A Theory of Afro-American Literary Criticism* (New York: Oxford University Press, 1988), 51.

[47]Waller also signifies by interpolating comments during instrumental solos, including his own; the signifying in these instances can relate either to aspects of the performance or to the music or text of the piece itself. An example of Waller's signifying on the music during one of his solos occurs in "I'm Crazy 'Bout My Baby" (13 March 1931, mx. 151417-3; see Transcription 5a, mm. 60–80); an example of his signifying on the text of a piece may be found in "The Darktown Strutters' Ball" (3 November 1939, mx. 043350-1). Here, Waller calls out "Sepia Town—ahh, look at my little bronze body!" The irony inherent in the reference to his body as "little" is humorous in an obvious sense, but Waller's use of "sepia" and "bronze," in the context of a song whose central image ("Darktown Strutters") is already freighted with racial overtones, carries broader implications. In one sense, Waller is signifying on racial stereotyping, substituting the sophisticated (and coded) "Sepia Town" for the less elegant euphemism "Darktown." "Bronze" is likewise a code word

Amending Texts

In amending text, Waller adopts two somewhat different forms of verbal reconstruction. First, he replaces simple words with complex equivalents. Thus he parodies the title line of "Your Feet's Too Big" by changing it to "your pedal extremities are colossal." (The vaudeville stage provides antecedents for this form of linguistic play.)[48] In a similar vein, the title line of "I'm Crazy 'Bout My Baby" becomes in Waller's rendition "I'm exasperated 'bout my offspring," though in this example, the new text transforms—indeed, in some sense reverses—the meaning of the original.[49] An even more complex approach to parody through text manipulation may be embedded in Waller's claim that "exuberance is the spontaneity of life," perhaps a riff on the cliché "variety is the spice of life." Waller's version expands on the original, but unlike the paraphrase of "Your Feet's Too Big," the nouns Waller uses are not synonyms for the words they replace; his language is captivating, but his meaning is obscure. He seems to be engaging in a form of corrosive word play that undermines the cognitive value of the original texts. Waller's words here, as in some of his other nonsensical witticisms, sound like a sophisticated recasting of the epigram on which they are based, serving to mock learned verbal affectations. His rendering of the epigram blurs its meaning, while at the same time inflating it.[50]

Second, Waller amends text in order to reverse its purpose—to change, for example, a bland but sincere appeal into assertive, humorous satire. Waller's 1936 recording of Billy Mayhew's Tin Pan Alley song "It's a Sin to Tell a Lie"[51] affords an illustration. The musical structure of the chorus conforms to a standard Tin Pan Alley format—four eight-measure sections in an ABAC sequence—and the lyrics follow a simple rhyme scheme (see example 9). One performance strategy for animating this lyric would be to take it at face value, articulating melody and text as testimony to the song's earnest blend of desire and anxiety. Billie Holiday's 1942 recording with Teddy Wilson's Orchestra,[52] for example, genuinely—if improbably—ennobles the sentiments implied by the text. Waller, however, takes an altogether different approach (see example 10).[53]

While Mayhew's lyric in its original form explains why lying should be considered sinful, Waller's addition of the proactive final line adds another layer of meaning that may not be readily apparent. In her collection of African-American folklore *Mules and*

---

for "dark," which in this context constitutes an affirmative signifier. Two contemporary films with African-American casts use the word in their titles: *The Bronze Buckaroo* (1939) and *The Duke Is Tops* (1938, starring Ralph Cooper and Lena Horne), which was also known as *The Bronze Venus* (presumably a take-off on *Blonde Venus* of 1933). In addition, Ralph Cooper became known as the "bronze Bogart" as a result of the widespread popularity of *Dark Manhattan* (1937), in which he starred. (The editor gratefully acknowledges the assistance of Margaret McFadden, Assistant Professor of American Studies at Colby College, who generously supplied the foregoing information.) At the time Waller recorded "The Darktown Strutters' Ball," then, the term "bronze" would have resonated with his African-American audience as Hollywood's version of the ideal African-American image, and he would have been understood as applying a positive racial characteristic to himself.

[48]See Gavin Jones, *Strange Talk, The Politics of Dialect Literature in Gilded Age America* (Berkeley: University of California Press, 1999), chapter 6.

[49]See Machlin, *Stride,* 37–38.

[50]Similar forms of linguistic sabotage are found in other cultural contexts. Lewis Carroll, for example, creates in Humpty Dumpty a character whose verbal antics bear a noticeable resemblance to Waller's: " 'When *I* use a word,' Humpty Dumpty said, in rather a scornful tone, 'it means just what I choose it to mean—neither more nor less.' " Lewis Carroll, *Through The Looking-Glass and What Alice Found There* (New York: Rand McNally & Company, 1916), 186.

[51]Fats Waller and His Rhythm, 5 June 1936, mx. 101667-1; music and lyrics by Billy Mayhew; first published by Bregman, Vocco & Conn, Inc., 1936.

[52]Billie Holiday, accompanied by Teddy Wilson and His Orchestra, 10 February 1942, mx. 32407-1.

[53]As for other vocal transcriptions in this volume, braces { } surrounding text indicate that it is growled and underlining indicates exaggerated, distorted, or otherwise modified pronunciation (see Apparatus: Text); *italic type* here indicates the text was spoken.

Example 9. Lyrics for Billy Mayhew's "It's a Sin to Tell a Lie"

> Be sure it's true when you say "I love you;" it's a sin to tell a lie.
> Millions of hearts have been broken, just because these words were spoken.
> I love you, yes I do, I love you; if you break my heart, I'll die.
> So be sure it's true when you say "I love you;" it's a sin to tell a lie.

Example 10. Transcription of Waller's vocal rendition of "It's a Sin to Tell a Lie" as performed by Fats Waller and His Rhythm, 5 June 1936, mx. 101667-1

> Be sure it's true when you say "I love you;" it's a sin to tell a lie.
> *Millions of hearts have been broken, {yes,} yes; just because these words were spoken—do you know the words that were spoken? Here 'tis:*
> *I love you, I love you, I love you, I love you, hah-hah-hah!* Yes, but if you break my {heart,} I'll break your {jaw,} and then I'll die.
> So {be sure} it's true when you say I love you, *hah-hah! It's a sin to tell a lie. Now get on out there and tell your lie—what is it?*

Men (1935), Zora Neale Hurston discloses a sense of the noun "lie" (as well as of the verb) that most white Americans would not have known. She relates that she had traveled to her hometown of Eatonville, Florida in order, as she explained to friends, "to collect some old stories and tales." In response to this statement of purpose, one of the townsfolk asks, "What you mean, Zora, them big old lies we tell when we're jus' sittin' around here on the store porch doin' nothin'?"[54] Here, then, the phrase "tell a lie" connotes not deception in a moral sense, but rather narrative, an aesthetic concept central to performance in all spheres of African-American culture—not only in storytelling, but in blues and jazz soloing as well.[55]

Seen in this context, Waller's added line is double-coded, projecting fundamentally different meanings to distinct audiences. Taken at face value, his injunction ("Now get on out there and tell your lie—what is it?") contradicts the moral implicit in the title ("It's a sin to tell a lie"). Waller assumes that the object of his affection will ultimately lie, whatever the substance of that lie might be, thus neutralizing any emotional consequences the lie might have had for him. This much would be apparent even to uninitiated members of an audience. But Hurston's story suggests another interpretation, aimed at an African-American audience. This alternative, unrelated to the sense of Mayhew's original, fits the way a small jazz ensemble works: the leader (Waller) simply encourages his soloists to play well—to get on out there and tell their stories.

In other respects, Mayhew's text presents fertile ground for satire, and Waller plows this ground with two well-honed tools. He adopts a variety of vocal timbres and inflections, and he embellishes the text by adding new words and indulging in verbal asides. Both of these signifying elements serve to ridicule the narrator's vulnerability (the very quality Holiday emphasizes) to the point of reversing the song's meaning. Waller opens his performance with a brief instrumental introduction followed by a lively stride piano version of the thirty-two-measure chorus that sets the stage for farce. In the second chorus, Waller sings the text in his amended version, but, though his opening delivery

---

[54]Zora Neale Hurston, *Mules and Men* (New York: Harper & Row, Publishers, Inc., 1990; originally published by J. B. Lippincott, Inc., 1935), 8.

[55]This meaning is confirmed by the *Dictionary of American Regional English,* ed. Frederic G. Cassidy and Joan Houston Hall (Cambridge: Harvard University Press, 1996), which cites several additional sources for this specific usage on p. 346.

is straightforward, by the end of the first line he is indulging in burlesque. Savaging the title words with an overly resonant bass timbre that oozes pretension, he lets the word "lie" disintegrate into an extended, adenoidal grunt, and then reestablishes a pretentious tone for the next line ("Millions of hearts . . ."). Unadorned, the phrase evokes sympathy for those who have been deceived in love, implying that widespread suffering can be caused by a minor infraction. But Waller mocks that notion by striking an air of pontification; without changing a word of the lyric, he undermines its moral authority through comic (and deforming) inflection. He exaggerates his delivery of the crucial third line of the stanza by repeating the phrase "I love you" a total of four times in a sequence that descends rapidly in pitch. Repetition and bluster serve the purpose of satire here, but to drive home his point, Waller adds a burst of stylized laughter at the end of the line—a malicious yet infectious "hah-hah-hah!" By stepping outside the role of protagonist and commenting on the text in this fashion, Waller emphasizes his emotional distance from the sentiment of the song.

This essential element of signifying—critiquing the text being performed within the context of the performance itself—characterizes Waller's added commentary to the text as well as the inflections he uses to color it. Waller compacts the second half of the second line rhythmically ("just because these words were spoken"), hastening over it so that he can create a space to interpolate the rhetorical question, "Do you know the words that were spoken?" He thus deftly shifts the singer's role from anxious but passive observer to aggressive and active inquisitor. But instead of issuing an invitation to dialogue, he answers his own question himself ("I love you"). Waller signifies on the third line of the stanza ("If you break my heart, I'll die") by inserting "I'll break your jaw and then," playing the figurative meaning of the verb "break" against its literal meaning. In a sense, this pun constitutes the rhetorical equivalent of Waller's stride piano tricks—a verbal embellishment with a mocking thrust. By recontextualizing the verb "break," Waller transforms the pain and resignation implied in the original text into a brutal, absurdly comic image.

Verbal Dueling

Satire of original texts, then, is one form that Waller's signifying takes. A second form consists of enacting a verbal duel, and, on occasion, Waller creates a particular comic persona especially for this purpose.[56] In "It's a Sin to Tell a Lie," the act of signifying implies a partner to whom the repartee is directed, but in a solo performance such as Waller's, no actual exchange of banter can take place. "I Can't Give You Anything But Love,"[57] another Tin Pan Alley song performed by Waller, is also written as if directed to an absent lover. The arrangement for one of Waller's recorded versions of this tune, however, provides for two singers (see example 11, first chorus).[58] While each presumably was assigned a separate chorus in this performance, the potential for dialogue is inherent in the arrangement. Donning his signifying persona, Waller continually interrupts his colleague's singing during the first of the two choruses, transforming her solo

[56]To underscore the presence of this persona, Waller could refer to himself in the second or third person, thereby inviting members of the audience to share his critique and turning them into co-conspirators. Waller, who was about six feet tall and often weighed over 250 pounds, reportedly began at least one of his solo concerts by twirling the top of a small piano stool, carefully settling himself on it, and archly asking "Is you all on there, Fatsy Watsy?" (Kirkeby, *Ain't Misbehavin'*, 201; see also Waller and Calabrese, *Fats Waller*, 57).

[57]Dorothy Fields (words) and Jimmy McHugh (music), Mills Music, 1928. Barry Singer speculates, with considerable justification, that this song was actually written by Waller and his long-time lyricist, Andy Razaf (Barry Singer, *Black and Blue: The Life and Lyrics of Andy Razaf* [New York: Schirmer Books, 1992], 209–11). See also Paul S. Machlin, "Fats Waller Composes: The Sketches, Drafts, and Lead Sheets in the Institute of Jazz Studies Collection," *Annual Review of Jazz Studies, 1994–1995* (Lanham, Md. and London: The Scarecrow Press, 1996), 2.

[58]Fats Waller and His Rhythm, 3 November 1939, mx. 043351-1.

rendition into an adversarial duet. His commentary restructures the arrangement, resulting in two utterly different versions of the lyric. The first is a collaboration that combines a straight delivery of the text with a signifying commentary, while the second is a solo in which Waller's signifying involves both text alteration and tone manipulation.

Waller's partner in this 1939 recording is the cabaret singer Una Mae Carlisle, who in the early 1930s, according to Waller's son Maurice, had been invited by Waller to appear on his Cincinnati radio show. They apparently developed a close relationship, but by 1933 the relationship had cooled considerably, even to the point of outright aversion.[59] Certainly, a palpable tension between the two may be heard in the recording. Perhaps it is fed by the genuine enmity between Waller and Carlisle, by this time long-standing, or perhaps it arises because the song offers an ideal arena for staging an archetypal gender conflict. In either case, the extreme contrast in the two singers' styles gives voice to the tension embedded in the performance. Where Carlisle, who sings the melodic line almost exactly as written, uses legato articulation, smooth vocal transitions, and large note values in a swung but not eccentric rhythm, Waller prefers a more staccato approach to the words and articulation, sharply accented attacks, abrupt shifts in timbre, and short notes in unpredictable rhythmic patterns—all conversational in effect. This vocal clash creates what, in African-American aesthetic terms, is a classic confrontation: the juxtaposition of "cool" and "hot" values.[60]

Example 11. "I Can't Give You Anything But Love," Dorothy Fields (words) and Jimmy McHugh (music), Mills Music, Inc., © 1928; lyrics as performed by Una Mae Carlisle and Fats Waller as performed by Fats Waller and His Rhythm, 3 November 1939, mx. 043351-1

FIRST CHORUS (DUET)

CARLISLE	WALLER
I can't give you anything but love, Baby. That's the only thing I've plenty of, oh Baby.	
	Don't you tell me; yes, what am I supposed to do?
Dream awhile,	
	Yes—
Scheme awhile,	
	You're wrong.
You're sure to find	
	That's what you think I'm sure to find.
Happiness	
	{*Um hmm—*}

[59] Waller and Calabrese, *Fats Waller,* 108–10.

[60] This juxtaposition has been established by art historian Robert Farris Thompson as an essential element of several aspects of West African art (notably in the masks of the Yoruba people) and, by extension, of African-American art. See Thompson's "African Art and Motion," in *The Jazz Cadence of American Culture,* ed. Robert G. O'Meally (New York: Columbia University Press, 1998), 331, 364. (In the context of jazz history, of course, these two adjectives are used somewhat differently, referring to specific musical styles.)

Example 11. continued

(Carlisle)

And I guess,
All those things you're sure to pine for.
Gee, I'd love to see you lookin' swell,
Baby,

(Waller)

Well my tailor's waitin' right outside the door,
He can keep me lookin' swell, I ain't playin'.

(Carlisle)

Diamond bracelets Woolworth's doesn't sell, my little Baby.

(Waller)

I never had a diamond bracelet in my life; what do I want it for?

(Carlisle)

'Til that lucky day you know darn well, ooo, Baby,

(Waller)

What happens? What goes on in here?

(Carlisle)

That I can't give you anything but love.

Second Chorus (Solo)

(Waller)

Come here, let me tell you somethin':
{I} can't dish out anything but love, {Ba'!}
{That's} the {on}ly thing {I've got} plenty {of, Baby}.
You talkin' 'bout dreamin' awhile, {schemin' awhile,} you're sure to find
Happiness, and I guess, all those fine Arabian things your little heart pines for, yes.
Skip 'em! I'd love to see you lookin' swell.
{Diamond bracelets?} Woolworth ain't got no business sellin' 'em; you can go to, go (t') ah, well, ah well, well, well, Ho—
'Til that lucky day, you know {darn} well, well Baby,
I ain't dishin' out nothin', ain't gettin' {off} on {nothin' but love.}
How's that Babes? There's your diamonds.

Carlisle's serene rendition would be convincing on its own terms, but Waller seeks to undermine the text's sincerity, creating a skirmish at every turn.[61] Some of his routines are playful; others reflect the antagonism (either genuine or staged) between the

[61] As with "It's a Sin to Tell a Lie," Billie Holiday, in her recording of "I Can't Give You Anything But Love," deepens the sense of pathos inherent in the original lyric (Billie Holiday accompanied by Teddy Wilson and His Orchestra, a septet that included Benny Goodman playing under the name of John Jackson, 19 November 1936, mx. B-20293-1). Though Holiday and Carlisle are singers of a very different kind, their interpretations suggest that they both accept at face value the sincere intentions implied by the text.

personas of the two singers. Waller initiates the conflict between sincere and subversive discourse with a gentle taunt ("Don't you tell me"). He thus assumes the traditional role of a blues singer's accompanist, an integral part of his musical past, by filling in the available space at the end of a phrase after the singer has completed her line. Verbally and musically, Waller's commentary belongs to the realm of call and response. But he soon abandons his reactive position, asserting control over Carlisle's monologue by asking, "What am I supposed to do?" In its original context, the next line ("Dream awhile") seems a romantic reverie. Now, however, we hear it as a limp answer to Waller's question. Moreover, the positions originally held by the two singers in the call-and-response hierarchy are now reversed. Waller ratchets up the intensity of the exchange further by flatly contradicting Carlisle—"You're wrong."

In the second half of the verse, Waller increases both the pace and the amount of his banter, intensifying the conflict. When Carlisle sings "Gee, I'd love to see you lookin' swell," he sabotages these words by taking them literally, transforming her generic wish into a concrete scenario ("Well, my tailor's waiting right outside the door"). This tactic parallels his approach to reinterpreting the verb "break" in "It's a Sin to Tell a Lie," in which he changes or reverses the meaning of the text without altering the words. Carlisle's observation that Woolworth's (a chain of American stores that sold only inexpensive merchandise) does not sell diamonds belabors the obvious: although she would like to see her lover "lookin' swell" by giving him a costly gift, she can't afford to.[62] Waller's retort ("I never had a diamond bracelet in my life, what do I want it for?") turns the metaphor against Carlisle, belittling the token she offers as proof of her love. On one level, these exchanges amount to fast-paced banter; on another, they suggest a struggle for control in the relationship. Indeed, this form of contention is another expression of signifying.

Waller introduces his own chorus of "I Can't Give You Anything But Love" as if about to tell a story, or perhaps lecture an errant child (see example 11, second chorus). Waller's tone from the outset signals his intent to dispel any romantic illusions created by the lyrics or Carlisle's straightforward rendition. Within the framework of the song, Waller takes aim at the notion that a lack of money can somehow be equated with true romantic feeling. His performance transforms the original text's sentimental declaration of love into a pointed debunking of it. Many details in the performance contribute to this transformation: the sharply articulated syllable "Ba' " (pronounced "bay") replaces Carlisle's languorous, drawn out "baby"; a mocking sigh inflects the word "happiness"; and the phrase "you talking about dreamin' awhile" demotes Carlisle's "dream awhile" into idle chatter. For the rhetorical climax at the midpoint of the chorus, Waller revises the phrase "all those things you've always pined for," transforming it into "all those fine Arabian things your little heart pines for, yes." What Waller meant by "those fine Arabian things" may not be immediately clear, but the arch tone of his delivery suggests the phrase carries a coded subtext. Certainly, this was not the first time the exotic Near East had surfaced in his show business career. Perhaps the image was prompted by an event in his past (Waller appeared as "Ali Baba, the Egyptian Wonder" at the Kentucky Club opposite Duke Ellington in 1924, where he apparently clowned in a jeweled turban[63]) or by specific songs in his repertoire. Shortly before the "I Can't Give You Anything But Love" recording date, he had recorded two songs with an Arabian motif in their titles ("Abdullah"[64] and "The Sheik of Araby"[65]). The text for

[62]At this point, the issue of gender role reversal raised by Carlisle's performance of these lyrics—intended to be sung by a male—becomes acute. The intensity of Waller's animus suggests that his antagonism, perhaps even a need to assert power over Carlisle in this struggle, may in some measure have been prompted by this reversal.

[63]Waller and Calabrese, *Fats Waller,* 56–57.

[64]Fats Waller and His Rhythm, New York, 10 August 1939, mx. 041531-1.

[65]Fats Waller, His Rhythm And His Orchestra, New York, 12 April 1938, mxx. 022434-1 and 022434-2; also, with an unnamed ensemble, New York, 7 August 1939, ZZ 2143. This latter recording was a transcription disc for radio broadcast made at the Bronx, New York studios of Associated Transcriptions.

the latter includes the suggestive couplet "At night when you're asleep / into your tent I'll creep." Moreover, on Waller's second take of "The Sheik of Araby" for Victor, during the trumpet solo (probably by Herman Autrey, whom Waller identifies as "one of them Georgia Arabians"), he interpolates spoken commentary with sexual overtones: "Get on a camel? Not now—I ain't used to ridin' between humps!"[66] For Waller, then, "fine Arabian things" may well have carried a sexual charge.[67] As if to deliver a coup de grace, however, Waller devises the perfect moral about-face: he admonishes his lover and his audience to banish whatever salacious images he may have conjured up with the order to "Skip 'em!"

Waller concludes his subversion of this lyric by reinterpreting the text's reference to diamonds, treating the image not as a metaphor for the value of love but rather as a lesson in practical economics. Sweeping aside the dime-store diamonds, he dismisses the supposed object of his affection by telling her to go to hell (though he coyly substitutes a euphemism for the phrase, which nevertheless fits the rhyme scheme). Yet though his animosity thus far is unmistakable, Waller reverses himself at the last possible moment with a final musical trope on the lyrics—one unexpectedly at odds with the belligerence of his dialogue. He accompanies his last comment ("There's your diamonds") with an A♭-major sixth chord that he repeats in a rising sequence in the upper register of the right hand (m. 69). These high, crystalline chords are Waller's jewels, evanescent perhaps, but just as beautiful as the bracelets not sold by Woolworth's.

Parody

In his third form of signifying, Waller employs musical allusions and parody both to acknowledge certain styles of classical music and to critique the privileged position of classical music in American culture. The performance which illuminates this dual intent most comprehensively is his 13 May 1941 solo recording of "Honeysuckle Rose," subtitled "à la Bach, Beethoven, Brahms, and Waller" (Transcription 6b).[68] In this remarkable realization of the song, he parodies European classical music by troping his own tune with gestures that seem intended to suggest the language of the composers cited in the subtitle. Through these musical inventions, Waller celebrates his knowledge of classical music while at the same time demonstrating both compositional skill and virtuosity in the stride piano style. He also critiques classical music by sometimes exaggerating its gestural formulas. Waller's emphasis on the parallels between his art and that of the classical masters he parodies thus attacks the distinction between high and low culture, art music and popular entertainment music. He seeks not only to elevate stride as art, but more specifically, to undermine the hierarchy used so frequently in America to reinforce racial and class prejudice.

The choice of "Honeysuckle Rose" is by no means arbitrary, for the tune is arguably Waller's most popular and enduring song—a favorite with jazz and popular musicians alike.[69] The 1941 recording is one of four Waller made in the studio. The other three

[66]Fats Waller, His Rhythm And His Orchestra, New York, 12 April 1938, mx. 022434-2.

[67]The innuendo is certainly clear in Andy Razaf's lyric for "My Handy Man Ain't Handy No More" from Lew Leslie's show *Blackbirds of 1930:* "I used to brag about my Handy Man's technique, Around the house he was a perfect indoor sheik, But now 'The spirit's willing but the flesh is weak' "; the song was sung in the show by Ethel Waters (Singer, *Black and Blue,* 249). Although Waller apparently never recorded this tune, Kirkeby says that he performed it at the Hotfeet Club in 1931 (Kirkeby, *Ain't Misbehavin',* 151).

[68]Fats Waller, 13 May 1941, mx. 063890-1.

[69]Richard Crawford and Jeffrey Magee, *Jazz Standards on Record, 1900–1942; A Core Repertory* (Chicago: Center for Black Music Research, 1992), reports fifty-two recordings of the tune by jazz musicians, tied with Gershwin's "I Got Rhythm" for eleventh place on a list of ninety-seven tunes that were recorded twenty times or more.

include two performed by a sextet called "Fats Waller and His Rhythm" (7 November 1934 and 9 April 1937, though there were slight differences in personnel on the two dates), and one titled "A Jam Session at Victor," recorded on 31 March 1937 by a small group that featured Bunny Berigan and Tommy Dorsey. In addition, Waller played "Honeysuckle Rose" in many radio broadcasts, on film, on transcription discs, on private recordings, and in concert. Recordings of some of these performances have surfaced, either in their original format or as reissues,[70] so that at this writing, thirteen different Waller performances of "Honeysuckle Rose" are known to survive. Indeed, jazz critic and scholar Dan Morgenstern has speculated that Waller "must have played this tune every working day of his life."[71] Yet none of the recorded performances resembles any of the others, a point Morgenstern makes about all Waller recordings, successive takes included.[72] And none is even close to "Honeysuckle Rose, à la Bach, Beethoven, Brahms, and Waller."

The original grouping of the three European composers in the alliterative triumvirate of the subtitle ("the Three B's") has been traced to the nineteenth-century German conductor Hans von Bülow, who proclaimed: "I believe in Bach the Father, Beethoven the Son, and Brahms, the Holy Ghost of music."[73] The association of these composers as icons of European classical music is deeply embedded in American popular culture. Thus, linking their names to Waller's signals not only a generalized parody of the world of high art, but a musical argument placing stride in this artistic realm. Even though Waller apparently made no recordings of European piano literature, shortly after his death his longtime collaborator Andy Razaf gave persuasive testimony that he could play it: "He knew Brahms, Liszt and Beethoven as well as he knew jazz, and often discussed and analyzed their work."[74] Waller himself also once claimed to have studied Bach,[75] and he peppers his variations with formal gestures that appear to have been modeled on those found in the works of these three European composers specifically.[76] Perhaps he meant the recording's subtitle as a generic invocation of classical music, but it is also possible that he intended to refer directly to the works of Bach, Beethoven, and Brahms.

Waller would also, of course, have been conversant with the venerable practice of reinterpreting works from the standard European concert repertoire in a jazz idiom.[77] In "Honeysuckle Rose, à la Bach, Beethoven, Brahms, and Waller," however, he accomplishes something quite different. He reverses the approach of ragging the classics by using his own tune, a certified and familiar jazz standard, as the basis for a set of preconceived extemporizations inspired by his notions of European practice. Waller

---

[70]One of these reissues appears on a disc in the New World set of recordings titled ". . . and then we wrote . . ." (New World Records 272, Recorded Anthology of American Music, Inc., 1977). However, it is incorrectly identified in the liner notes as a recording made on 2 August 1939. Waller made no recordings on that date; although he did record "Honeysuckle Rose" on 7 August 1939, the reissue on the New World disc is not that recording. Rather, the New World reissue is the recording Waller made on 11 March 1935 for Associated Transcriptions (see Transcription 6a).

[71]Dan Morgenstern, liner notes to *Fats Waller: "Oh, Mercy! Looka Here," His Piano . . . His Rhythm, 1935 & 1939,* Honeysuckle Rose Records (3-disc LP boxed set), HR 5001-3, n.d.

[72]Morgenstern, *Fats Waller: "Oh, Mercy! Looka Here."*

[73]Quoted in Nat Shapiro, *An Encyclopedia of Quotations About Music* (Garden City: Doubleday & Company, 1978), 43.

[74]Andy Razaf, "Fats Waller," *Metronome* 60:1 (January 1944): 16.

[75]"I consider the thorough bass foundation I got in the study of Bach the best part of my training" *Metronome* 52:2 (February 1936): 19.

[76]It should be emphasized, however, that any such correspondences do not imply quotation or even that Waller was familiar with particular pieces.

[77]He even recorded jazz versions of arias and ensembles from well-known operas, among them *Samson and Delilah, Faust, Martha,* and *Lucia di Lammermoor* (all recorded 20 November 1939 on 16-inch Langworth transcription discs).

apparently established the structural framework and colorful stylistic details of the performance before making the 1941 recording, so that "Honeysuckle Rose, à la Bach, Beethoven, Brahms, and Waller" differs in character both from his other recordings of the piece, and indeed from most of his recorded work. Waller thus offers a knowing commentary on the material of his own composition reinvented in what he took to be a classical idiom. An additional goal may also have been simply to lampoon pretension: the fourth composer cited is, after all, Waller himself.[78]

The opening gesture—a repeated five-note descending group in the right hand encompassing an octave and articulated over a sustained dominant pedal—lies easily under the hand in almost every major key, and it is one of Waller's basic tricks. After a brief pause, Waller initiates an extensive downward run; his delicately offhand execution of the passage, as well as its range and elaborate swirling character, suggest aspects of the pianism of Liszt and his disciples. In a jazz context, the passage also invokes the style of Art Tatum, whose virtuosity was widely recognized, and whom Waller greatly admired. In this sense, perhaps the gesture represents an attempt to signify on the younger and relatively unknown pianist by demonstrating an equivalent or even superior prowess in the kind of technical display usually associated with Tatum. Even from the very outset of his performance, then, Waller traces a fine line between sincerity and satire, homage and parody.

Waller's take on the verse of "Honeysuckle Rose," which follows the introduction, is also rhythmically free. But though his rubato approach continues the introduction's whimsical mood, using rolled chords, unpredictable changes in texture and line, short phrases, and pauses of irregular lengths at unexpected moments (m. 13), the simplicity of this passage provides a clear contrast to the bravura of the opening run. Waller also incorporates into the verse music the first gloss on classical style: the rolled chords that support the melodic line in measures 3–4 and 7–8 echo an articulation found in Brahms (e.g., the *Rhapsody,* op. 119 no. 4, mm. 93 ff.), as well as in the piano pieces of many other nineteenth-century European composers (see examples 12a/b).

The verse closes with a somewhat grandiose pronouncement: a rising arpeggio on a diminished triad (m. 14). A jazz listener would hear this flourish as preparation for the chorus to follow and might also expect that the chorus would be played in strict tempo.[79] Instead of establishing a rhythmic groove, however, Waller starts the first AABA chorus (mm. 15–41) with a rubato delivery of the A melody, measure by measure at first, and over a bass figure in contrary motion. The second eight-measure A section begins the same way, an octave higher. In the bridge (B), whose half-note melody usually marks a sharp contrast with the eighth-note motion of the other phrases, Waller accelerates the melodic pace to make it consistent with the rest of the chorus. The return of the A melody to round out the first chorus is supported by a strong bass line and broken-chord figures in the left hand.

Waller has now delivered a version of the thirty-two-measure chorus of his own tune—originally composed in a popular idiom—in a manner that evokes the classical tradition. The absence of strict tempo differentiates the performance from usual jazz procedure. In addition, by richly varying his first statement of the chorus, Waller has made listeners ready to hear "Honeysuckle Rose" in musical units as short as eight measures (instead of the anticipated full chorus length of thirty-two measures). Moreover, a flexible tempo gives Waller the freedom to draw on an intensely expressive

---

[78]Just as Hugues Panassié correctly perceived the humor in Waller's singing (see note 45), so also he suggested the importance of humor in Waller's playing (Kirkeby, *Ain't Misbehavin',* 157).

[79]By 1941, when this recording was made, some pianists—notably Tatum—were making a standard convention of beginning solo recordings with an out-of-tempo statement of the verse, and perhaps even the first chorus, before settling into a strict tempo for the rest of the choruses. Waller, however, followed that strategy only on certain occasions. See, e.g., note 33.

Example 12. Comparison of usage of rolled chords in Waller and Brahms

a. Thomas "Fats" Waller, "Honeysuckle Rose, à la Bach, Beethoven, Brahms, and Waller," mm. 3–8

b. Johannes Brahms, Rhapsody, op 119, no. 4, mm. 93–97

vocabulary of pianistic gestures and colors. His subsequent chorus variations capitalize on these innovative elements. Here, Waller seems to be testifying, is what might result from an encounter between "Honeysuckle Rose" and a classical composer (à la the Three B's) who understood jazz technique.

The first chorus variation (mm. 42–60) begins with the right hand playing a repeated four-note figure, closely related to the opening gesture of the introduction, while the left outlines the song's chord progression, sometimes in parallel tenths (example 13a, mm. 42-47). This section of Waller's performance makes only an oblique reference to the original music of "Honeysuckle Rose." The melodic line here has been subsumed by the figuration, resulting in a kind of passagework also found in Bach's Harpsichord Concerto in D minor, BWV 1052, mm. 28 ff. (example 13b). In the bridge (mm. 50–53, foreshortened, like the bridge of the opening chorus, to four measures from the usual eight), the right-hand rippling shifts to figuration that complements parallel block chords in the left hand. This kind of stratification may be found in a broad cross-section of European keyboard music; it appears in both Bach (*The Well-Tempered Clavier*, Prelude no. 12 in F minor, BWV 857, mm. 6–7), and Brahms (Intermezzo, op. 117, no. 2, mm. 1–4).

Example 13. Comparison of melodic figuration in Waller and Bach

a. Thomas "Fats" Waller, "Honeysuckle Rose, à la Bach, Beethoven, Brahms, and Waller," mm. 42–47

b. Johann Sebastian Bach, Concerto in D Minor, BWV 1052, first movement, mm. 28–33, harpsichord part

The second chorus variation (mm. 61–88) begins as a waltz pastiche that, after ten measures, gives way to a brief but rhapsodic extemporization on the tune (ultimately in duple meter), incorporating in measure 75 another reference to the melodic hook and the bass figure in the first measure of the opening chorus (m. 15). The bridge of this variation (mm. 79–82; again, only four measures) reduces the original melody to a pair of ascending quarter-note sequences, supported by broken tenths in the left hand that trace the same rising curve heard in the melodic sequences. Having thus refashioned each of its four sections in a distinctive style, Waller concludes the second chorus variation with a rhythmically and texturally more complex version of its second (A) section, in preparation for his final take on the tune.

The third and last chorus variation (mm. 89–117) begins with pure stride piano and, for the first time in this performance, an extended passage in strict tempo. Suddenly, Waller abandons his musing in a classical vein, reveling instead in the musical virtuosity of the idiom he made his own. The speed and precision of both his decorative right-hand figure and the bass pattern in the left hand (mm. 90–100) sweep aside the rhythmic ebb and flow that characterized the previous variations. They demonstrate, too, that stride playing requires no less facility and brilliance than the language of Bach, Beethoven, and Brahms. Indeed, the infectious joy and excitement sparked by Waller's playing here dispel the genteel atmosphere (though not the elegance) of the performance thus far. But Waller's parade of moods and styles is not quite over. In the bridge, he briefly reinstates the waltz (mm. 105–7), then deflates its grandiosity with an informal, even mocking, response (mm. 108–9). And his final A section manifests the mixed pedigree of the whole performance: a statement of the melody that starts in stride-based swing, accelerates, dissolves into an arpeggiated series of descending chords, pauses to establish the dominant harmony in preparation for the cadence, and concludes with a virtuosic flourish characteristic of nineteenth-century pianism (mm. 122–25).

Waller's signifying in "Honeysuckle Rose, à la Bach, Beethoven, Brahms, and Waller" informs both his conception and execution of the composition. By juxtaposing and interweaving central elements of fundamentally different musics—jazz and the European classics—Waller questions the notion that they must inhabit separate performance arenas. Indeed, he uses each style to comment on the other: the stride passage in the last variation demonstrates that virtuosity can be as essential to jazz as to European keyboard music, while the freedom of tempo and stylistic variety Waller borrows from the classical tradition enrich the expressive possibilities of this Tin Pan Alley and jazz standard. By implication, then, Waller argues for cultural parity between the two traditions and undermines the convention that mandates their separation. As with his other forms of signifying, he harnesses his subversive wit in service of a broader aesthetic goal.

Conclusion

Fats Waller's professional work was circumscribed by two world wars. His growth as an artist thus occurred during a time of gradual but significant economic and social change as well as intense technological progress in America. His career benefited not only from these developments, which resulted in increased performance opportunities for him (both live and in the studio), but also from recording companies' burgeoning interest in African-American music—an interest fueled principally by the profitability of recordings made by African-American musicians.

Waller's artistry is preserved in published and unpublished compositions, sketches, and, most of all, sound recordings. This volume contains a small (but representative) sample of his legacy of recorded work in transcription. Fixing these particular performances in written form provides an alternative means of studying Waller's music and documenting its riches. The transcriptions reveal in specific detail the elements of his superb technique—utmost accuracy at breathtaking speeds and crisp execution of figuration and embellishments—and the breadth and variety of his invention. They also help illuminate the relationship between his humor and the archetypal forms of African-American discourse from which it springs. Finally, they disclose how Waller's substantial resources as a performer enliven his compositions, and how his approach to composition affects his performances—that is, how performance and composition for Waller are interdependent. Ultimately, if these transcriptions sharpen a reader's sense of Waller's music as it unfolds in the recordings, they will have served their purpose. For Waller himself underscores the need to pay close attention to the performance: "Listen, can you stand me to tell you about it? Listen here . . ."[80]

[80]Thomas "Fats" Waller, "I'm Crazy 'Bout My Baby," 13 March 1931, mx. 151417-3, mm. 7–9.

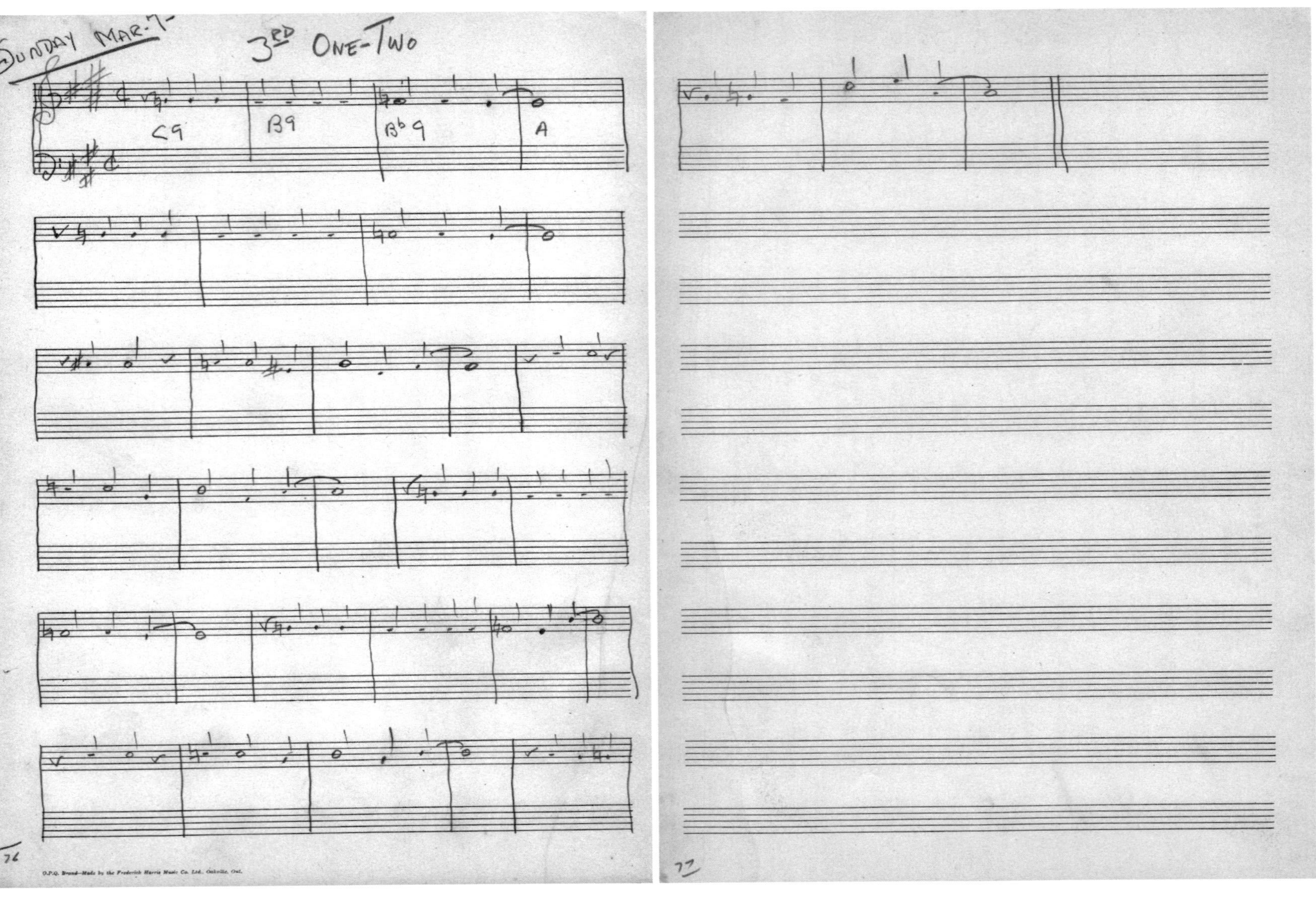

Plate 1. Thomas "Fats" Waller, "3rd One–Two" sketch for the musical *Early to Bed*, 1943. Courtesy of the Victor Amerling Collection, used by permission.

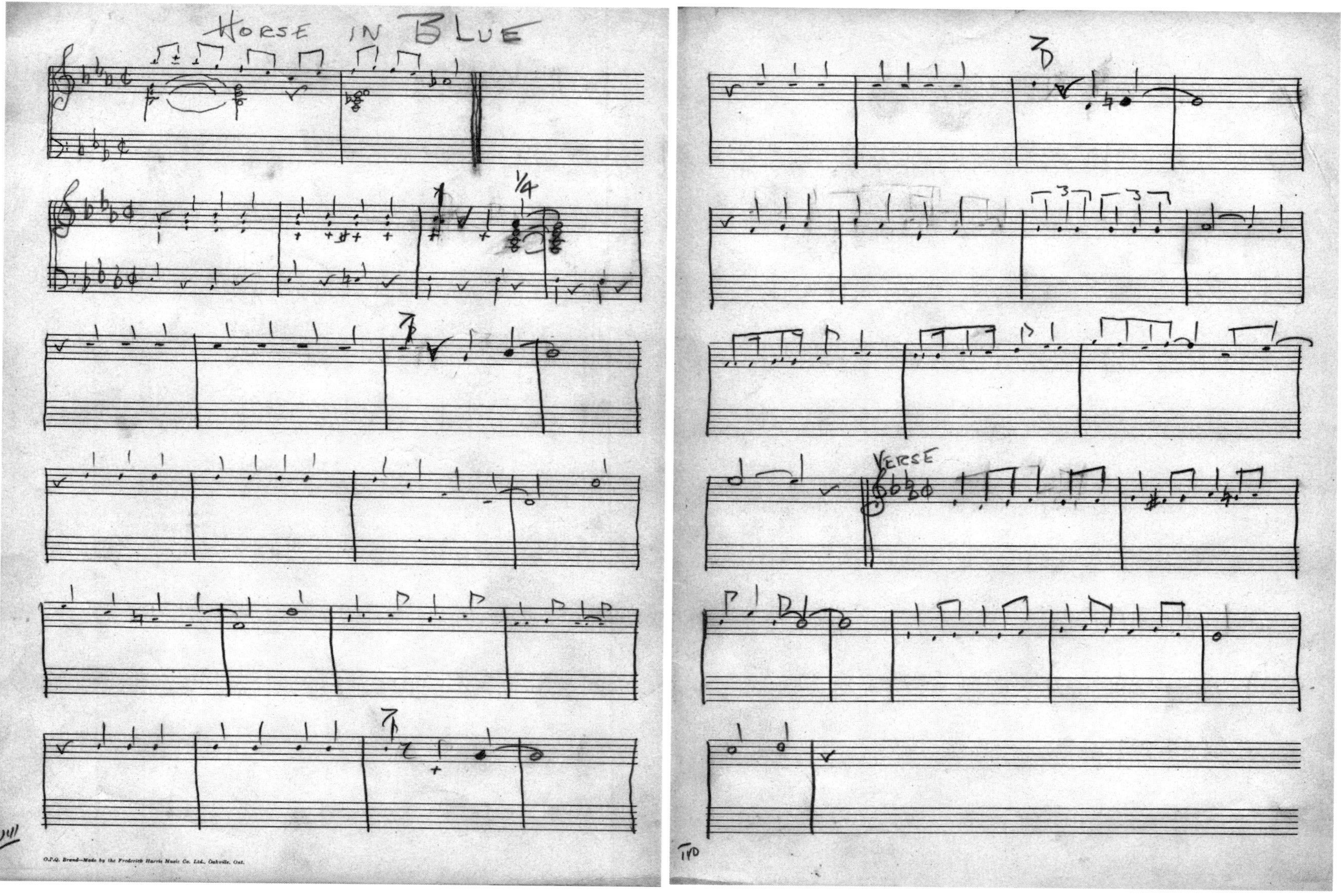

PLATE 2. Thomas "Fats" Waller, "Horse in Blue" sketch for the musical *Early to Bed*, 1943. Courtesy of the Victor Amerling Collection, used by permission.

PLATE 3. Thomas "Fats" Waller, "Wonderful/Horse in Blue" sketch for the musical *Early to Bed*, 1943. Courtesy of the Victor Amerling Collection, used by permission.

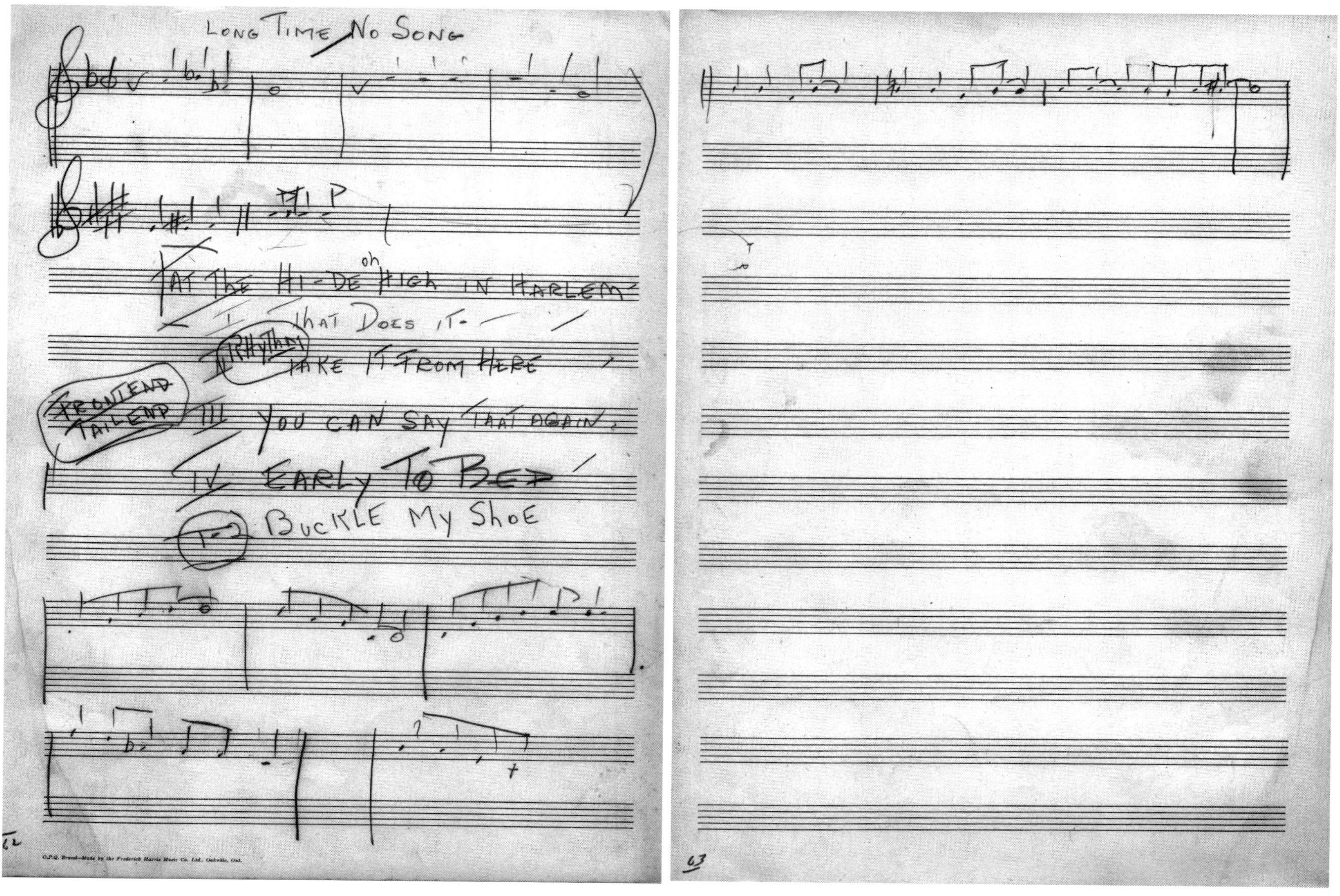

PLATE 4. Thomas "Fats" Waller, "Long Time No Song" sketch for the musical *Early to Bed*, 1943. Courtesy of the Victor Amerling Collection, used by permission.

Plate 5. Thomas "Fats" Waller, "That Does It/Nylons Bloom" sketch for the musical *Early to Bed*, 1943. Courtesy of the Victor Amerling Collection, used by permission.

Plate 6. Thomas "Fats" Waller, "2n" sketch for the musical *Early to Bed*, 1943. Courtesy of the Victor Amerling Collection, used by permission.

ALTERNATE TAKES, SAME INSTRUMENTATION

1. GLADYSE

Music. Thomas "Fats" Waller
Lyrics. None
Copyright. EU14961 (26 December 1929; unpublished)

Waller recorded two takes of "Gladyse" at the same remarkable session in August 1929 that produced several other solo piano masterpieces in the stride style. Indeed, Waller's sides from 1929, in general, provide ample evidence that he was at the very height of his technical and compositional powers, particularly with respect to the piano solos. Almost all of these performances embody the essential characteristics of his musical voice: boundless rhythmic energy and subtlety, technical agility, fertility of invention—especially in right hand embellishments—and a propulsive swing, generated by exceptionally subtle patterns of articulation in both the left and right hands, as well as judicious use of the damper pedal to strengthen or moderate accents. The rush of recording activity in this year also provides a strong indication of Waller's growing popularity as an artist, as well as the increasing economic importance of his output for the Victor Company as it expanded its catalogue.

Waller follows the same general dynamic and timbral scheme for both takes: a subdued, filigreed opening section, a more robust section of stride, a return for one

Take 1	**Take 2**
Introduction (mm. 1–2)	Introduction (mm. 1–4)
Chorus A (mm. 3–18)	Chorus A (mm. 5–20)
Chorus A′ (mm. 19–34)	Chorus A′ (mm. 21–36)
Transition (mm. 35–38)	Transition (mm. 37–40)
Chorus B (mm. 39–70)	Chorus B (mm. 41–72)
Chorus B′ (mm. 71–102)	Chorus B′ (mm. 73–104)
Introduction motive (mm. 103–4)	Introduction motive (mm. 105–6)
Chorus A (mm. 105–20)	Chorus A″ (mm. 107–22)
Chorus A* (mm. 121–36)	Chorus A* (mm. 123–38)
Coda (mm. 137–40)	Coda (mm. 139–42)

FIGURE 1. Comparison of form for two takes of "Gladyse." Uppercase letters (here A and B) represent distinct harmonic structures, each thirty-two measures long. Small uppercase letters refer to the individual phrases, each eight measures long, within a chorus. A prime symbol or asterisk following a letter, such as A′, shows that the new structure is a variant of the original identified by the letter.

sixteen-measure chorus to the opening sonority, a second section of stride, and a coda that evokes the delicacy of the introduction. The structure of the two takes differs only in the length of the introduction (see figure 1). Waller constructs the piece from two separate choruses which differ in length but which share the same basic AABA pattern of four phrases equal in length. In addition, for two choruses—B′ and A*—Waller welds together different characteristic musical elements of both choruses (the motivic material of Chorus A with the vigorous stride bass of Chorus B).[1]

The harmonic plan relies principally on key relationships based on the interval of a fourth (tonic and subdominant), and, indeed, much of the motivic material is based on this same interval. In and of itself, this factor suggests the influence of the blues on the composition of "Gladyse." The B chorus (in G major) not only begins in the right hand with the interval of a fourth (B♭ and E♭, the flatted fourth and sixth degrees of the scale) and returns to them often and prominently, but also, in the bridge, rocks back and forth harmonically between the subdominant (C major) modified by its flatted seventh and the tonic (G major) similarly modified. Thus, "Gladyse" may be taken as a measure of Waller's developing strength as a composer of stride piano music.

[1]See Paul S. Machlin, *Stride: The Music of Fats Waller* (Boston: Twayne Publishers, 1985), 20–21.

1a. GLADYSE

Recorded 2 August 1929 (mx. 49496-1)

Music by
Thomas "Fats" Waller

14
8
Ped.
[Ped.
Ped.
17
8
15ma
p
[Ped.
20
15ma
8
[Ped.
23
[Ped.
26
(8)
mp
Ped.

(8)
15ma
8
15ma
8
Ped.
Ped.
Ped.

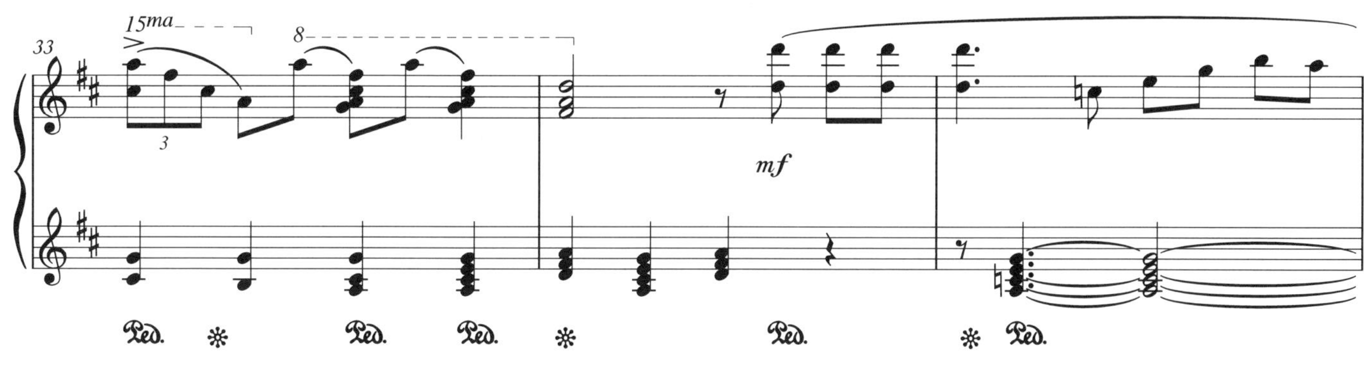

15ma
8
mf
Ped.
Ped.
Ped.
Ped.
Ped.

Ped.
Ped.
Ped.

= ca. 96–98
f
Ped.

Ped.
Ped.
Ped.

ossia
mf

61
f
64
67
70
mp
8
73
8
†

76
79
82
85
88
mf
[Ped. ❊ Ped. ❊ Ped. ❊ Ped. ❊ Ped. ❊ Ped. ❊]
Ped. ❊ [Ped. ❊ Ped. ❊]
[Ped. ❊ Ped. ❊ Ped. ❊ Ped. ❊] Ped. Ped.
❊ Ped. Ped. ❊ Ped. Ped. Ped. ❊ Ped. ❊
[Ped. ❊ Ped. ❊ Ped. ❊ Ped. ❊]

103
= ca. 100
p
8
3
[Ped. ※]

mp

121
8
f
3
Ped.
124
127
130
133

Commentary

Title. Gladyse
Source. Victor 78 rpm
Matrix number. 49496-1
Recording date. 2 August 1929
Reissue. "Fats" Waller Memorial, vol. 2 (RCA 731.054, 1971, LP)
Critical notes. M. 4, beat 1; m. 5, beat 1; RH: it is possible that the b‴ on the first eighth note of the triplet in both measures is a slip of the finger, but it occurs frequently enough as part of the gesture in this performance that Waller probably intended to play it, perhaps to color the resonant decay of the figure with a slight dissonance;

m. 12, beat 3, beat 4; m. 13, beat 1, RH: the e‴ on the second eighth note in each of these quarter note groups is probably an intentional dissonance rather than a slip of the finger (see also mm. 112–14 and m. 131);

m. 26, beat 3, RH: the grace note is articulated almost simultaneously with the eighth note;

m. 26, beat 3–m. 30, LH: the half notes are played very legato, but apparently without assistance from the damper pedal;

m. 59, beat 3; m. 60, beat 1; RH: Waller may have intended to play a″ as the top pitch of the chord on beat 3 of m. 59 instead of b♭″, constructing a melodic gesture parallel to that of m. 55; however, given that a similar discrepancy occurs in the next measure—that is, Waller strikes a″ on the downbeat of m. 60 instead of b♭″, as on the downbeat of m. 56—it seems likely that he has purposefully twisted the melodic contour of mm. 55–56 in order to vary it;

m. 71–78, RH: Waller provides a light, clear articulation for this phrase;

m. 74, beat 4, LH: the second eighth note of this beat should be d′; the c′ is probably a mistake;

m. 80, beat 2, LH: the second eighth note of this beat should be e; the f is probably a mistake;

m. 89, beat 2, RH: the dyad on the first eighth note is only very faintly audible in the recording;

m. 112, beat 4; m. 113, beat 2; m. 114, beat 1; RH: the three grace notes are articulated almost simultaneously with the eighth note (see mm. 12–13 and m. 131).

1b. GLADYSE

Recorded 2 August 1929 (mx. 49496-2)

Music by
Thomas "Fats" Waller

15
(8)
3
p
3
8
Ped.
Ped.
Ped.

19
8
3
15ma
8
3
Ped.

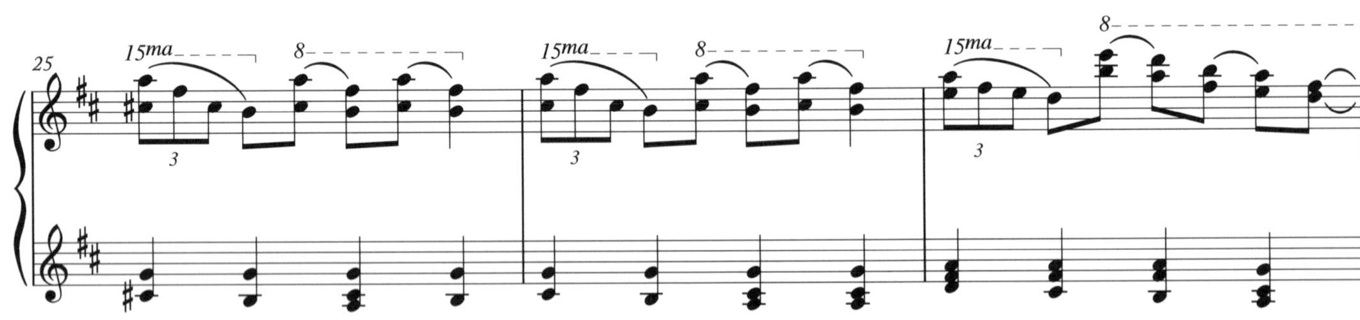
22
15ma
8
3
15ma
3
8

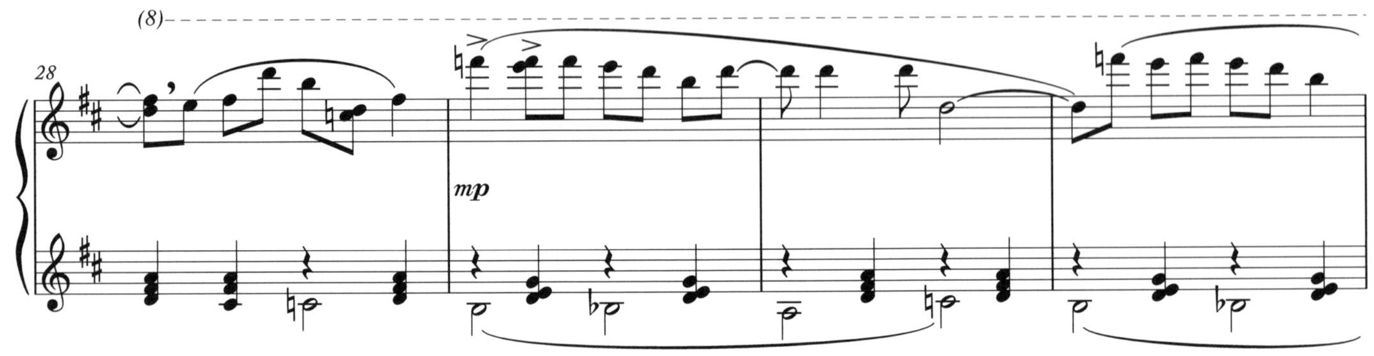
25
15ma
8
3
15ma
8
3
15ma
8
3
28
(8)
mp

(8)
15ma
8
p
mf
f
Ped.
†
††

49
mf
Ped. ✻

53
Ped. ✻ Ped. ✻
[Ped. Ped. Ped. Ped. Ped. Ped. ✻]

57
mf
[Ped. ✻]
Ped. ✻

61
[Ped. Ped. Ped. Ped.]
65
Ped. ✻ Ped. ✻ Ped. Ped. ✻ Ped. ✻

69
8
Ped. Ped. Ped. Ped. Ped. Ped.

73
(8)
mp
mf
8
mp

76
mf
Ped. Ped. Ped. Ped. Ped. Ped.

mp
mf

105
p
Ped.
109
112
mp
115
(8)
119

mf
f

Commentary

Title. Gladyse
Source. Victor 78 rpm
Matrix number. 49496-2 (unissued)
Recording date. 2 August 1929
Reissue. "Fats" Waller, "Complete Recordings," vol. 4 (RCA 741.086, May 1973, LP)
Critical notes. M. 5, beat 1, RH: Waller almost certainly intended this figure to be a triplet like the others on subsequent downbeats; his hand was probably late arriving at the upper octave;

m. 7, beat 3; m. 113, beat 3; LH: the lowest pitch of the chord sounds c′ but is a mistake; Waller would have intended to strike the pitch b (as in m. 11, for example);

m. 13–14, LH: the half notes here and in analogous passages for the left hand are played legato; if Waller enhanced this articulation with discreet use of the damper pedal, he was able to do so without disrupting the detached articulation of the right hand melody;

m. 15, beats 2, 3, 4, RH: the offbeat seconds may have been unintentional, but they assist in intensifying the percussive and jaunty pattern of accents for this gesture; this is true for the other manifestations of this embellishment in the performance as well;

m. 19, beat 1, RH: the first pitch of the triplet, b‴ and d♯‴, may have been a slip of the finger; Waller probably intended to strike a‴ and c♯‴;

m. 38, beats 1, 2, RH: Waller probably intended to continue the series of arpeggiated A-minor chords without the addition of g″ on the second eighth note of beat one and d″ on the first eighth note of beat two;

m. 43, beat 3, LH: the pitch should be D;

m. 63, beat 2, RH: the grace note is articulated almost simultaneously with the eighth note;

m. 63, beat 3, RH: at first hearing, the listener may construe this figure as a triplet; perhaps this aural illusion is created by the sound or placement of the grace note on the second eighth note of the previous beat; played at half speed, however, the recording reveals no evidence of a triplet;

m. 75, beat 1: because the eighth notes in the left hand are swung (as are all such eighth notes), the first and third eighth notes of the triplet on beat one in the right hand are sounded with the first and second eighth notes respectively of the left hand;

m. 100, beat 2, RH: Waller emphasizes the d♯″ of the first eighth note cluster and the e″ of the second eighth note dyad in order to outline, in conjunction with the first beat, an ascending chromatic line (d″–d♯″–e″);

m. 113, beat 3, LH: see note for m. 7;

m. 129, beat 3, LH: the GG is struck accidentally.

2. RUSTY PAIL BLUES

Title. Rusty Pail Blues (or Rusty Pail)
Music. Thomas "Fats" Waller
Lyrics. None
Copyright. E 664284 (2 May 1927)

The majority of Waller's pipe organ recordings, including his performances as a soloist, accompanist, and a member of an ensemble, were made in sessions that date from November 1926 to August 1929. Although it was still comparatively early in his career, by this time Waller was already an accomplished organist as well as a seasoned recording artist. The Estey Opus 2370 instrument on which he recorded (see Appendix) had been considerably refurbished in order to expand its range of repertoire. Nathaniel Shilkret, the Victor Company's Director of Light Music from 1915 to 1945, organized the unusually extensive session at which Waller played the two versions of "Rusty Pail Blues" transcribed here. Indeed, on this date (14 January 1927) Waller recorded no fewer than seven titles on pipe organ, making up to three takes for some of them; clearly, Shilkret intended to provide Waller ample opportunity to demonstrate both his artistry as a jazz organist and the expressive potential of the Victor Company's rebuilt instrument.

Waller's pipe organ recordings reveal the possibilities he discovered in this ostensibly ponderous instrument for the swinging rhythmic patterns and inventive melodic gestures intrinsic to jazz. Indeed, on at least one occasion Waller expressed a strong preference for the pipe organ over the piano: "I really love the organ. I can get so much more color from it than from the piano that it really sends me."[1] In the "Rusty Pail Blues" takes, as in his other pipe organ performances, Waller tends to contrast legato and staccato articulation within a single, often brief phrase in the right hand to help create the sense of brisk rhythmic propulsion essential to swing. He achieves this effect (and heightens the contrast between legato and staccato) by exploiting the organ's capability as a wind instrument both to extend a pitch without aural decay and to cut the sound off abruptly (see take one, Transcription 2a, mm. 24–28 and 53–60).[2]

One point of significant contrast between the two performances transcribed in this edition occurs at the end. In take one, Waller abandons the characteristic profile of the

[1]Nat Shapiro and Nat Hentoff, eds. *Hear Me Talkin' to Ya: The Story of Jazz as Told by the Men Who Made It* (New York: Rinehart & Co., 1955; reprinted New York: Dover Publications, 1966), 266.

[2]For a more complete discussion of the methods Waller uses to make the organ swing, as well as a detailed analysis of both the structure of "Rusty Pail Blues" and both performances, see Paul S. Machlin, *Stride: The Music of Fats Waller* (Boston: Twayne Publishers, 1985), 43–59.

A phrase almost entirely, substituting a series of dense, offbeat, diminished or seventh chords in the right hand. He articulates these with such an infectious crispness that it becomes instantly clear why his childhood friends, on hearing presumably similar passages in the Lincoln or Lafayette theaters in New York during Waller's teenage years, are reputed to have called out, "Make it rock, Fats!" In the third take (Transcription 2b), however, Waller adheres more closely to the original melodic line in the right hand, perhaps passing up the opportunity for a stomping conclusion in favor of a more rounded structure. To achieve this, Waller shifts back and forth between I^6 and a minor sixth on iv to extend the cadence through the final four measures.

The rebuilt Estey Organ in the Victor company's Camden (New Jersey) studio (a deconsecrated church) which Waller played for the recordings of "Rusty Pail Blues" had three keyboards (manuals) and three separate chests of stops: Great, Swell, and Solo. The specifications for the organ that are outlined in the relevant correspondence (see Apparatus) do not indicate which manual was connected to which chest, but if (as is probable) the design of the organ conformed to the usual assignment of keyboard to chest, the lowest manual would have been the Great organ, the middle manual would have been the Swell organ, and the top manual would have been the Solo organ. Since the specifications indicate that all stops for the Swell organ were "duplexed from the Great," it is probable that Waller's left hand played either the Great or the Swell manual, while his right hand played the Solo (or topmost) manual.

2a. RUSTY PAIL BLUES

Recorded 14 January 1927 (mx. 37362-1)

Music by
Thomas "Fats" Waller

(8)
17
mf
(8)
21
ossia
(8)
25
(8)
29
mf

(8)
33
f
p
(8)
37
mp
40
8
p
(8)
45

(8)
48
(8)
51
(8)
54
(8)
58

61
ff
8
66
(8)
f
71
ff
8
75
(8)
[ca. 𝅗𝅥 = 90]
[❊]
f
[a]

79
(8)
83
(8)
ff
87
(8)
91
(8)
mp

96
mf
100
[ca. 𝅗𝅥 = 92]
104
†
108
8
mp
†

112
(8)
116
(8)
120
(8)
124
(8)
mp

128
mf
132
(8)
ff
135
(8)
138
(8)
senza rit.

Commentary

Title. Rusty Pail Blues
Source. Victor 78 rpm
Matrix number. 37362-1 (unissued)
Recording date. 14 January 1927
Reissue. "Fats" Waller: Young Fats at the Organ, 1926–1927 (RCA 741.052, July 1972, LP)

Critical notes. M. 1, tempo: there is a gradual, almost imperceptible, increase in tempo in this performance; the tempos cited at mm. 77 and 101 indicate the pace Waller achieved when he reached those measures (rather than the sudden establishment of new tempos);

m. 13, beat 1, RH: the bar accent (lunga) over the first pitch of the measure (f‴) is intended to indicate a pitch held for its full value; it is also possible that Waller was able to add the sense of accent through use of the "second touch" feature of this Estey organ's keyboard (see Appendix);

m. 16, beat 4; m. 17, beat 1; RH: presumably this grace-note gesture was accomplished by sliding the thumb from g♯′ to a′;

m. 37–38: the change in timbre indicated by the asterisk above the staff here may be due only to the change in octave register from m. 37 to m. 38;

m. 38, beat 1; m. 39, beat 1: the left hand plays even eighth notes against the swung eighths of the right hand, producing a two against three rhythmic pattern;

m. 60–61: the change in timbre here is so sudden that it was probably accomplished by shifting from one manual to another;

m. 77, beat 3, LH: it is possible Waller strikes a B♭ in the pedal, but if so, it would have been a mistake;

m. 110–12, beat 1, RH: Waller articulates the gesture on the first beat with an almost imperceptible break between the first and second pitches—not enough to transcribe it with a rest (see m. 120), but the break is more noticeable than in the other articulations of this figure;

m. 126, beat 2, RH: the grace note is articulated simultaneously with the eighth note.

2b. RUSTY PAIL BLUES

Recorded 14 January 1927 (mx. 37362-3)

Music by
Thomas "Fats" Waller

(8)
mf
p
8
mf
p
(8)
mp

(8)
31
(8)
34
37
p
40

8
45
3
3
3
3
3
3
3
3
48
(8)
3
3
51
3
54
8

58
(8)
mf
62
66
[❊]
8
70
(8)

(8)
sub. pp
mf
8

90
(8)
94
(8)
98
(8)
102
(8)

106
111
8
(8)
115
119
(8)
sub. f

123
127
131
135
senza rit.
3

Commentary

Title. Rusty Pail Blues
Source. Victor 78 rpm
Matrix number. 37362-3
Recording date. 14 January 1927
Reissue. "Fats" Waller: Young Fats at the Organ, 1926–1927 (RCA 741.052, July 1972, LP)

Performance notes. Waller apparently does not articulate pitches on the pedal board in a consistent pattern or duration, except that he seems to favor legato (hence, transcribed in half notes) for half-step motion.

Critical notes. M. 21, beat 2: the clear dynamic shift that occurs between the second and third beats of this measure is probably the result of a registration change instituted by a coupler button or plunger, or by changing manuals; Waller probably intended to make this shift between the first and second beats of m. 20, just before the beginning of the new phrase;

m. 38: the change in timbre for this measure is probably the result of the octave shift rather than a change in registration;

m. 62, beat 3, LH: Waller makes the slightest break in the legato articulation of this line between the f and the d;

mm. 121–25; mm. 129–33; m. 134, beats 3–4; LH: the quarter note chords are still staccato, but slightly broader—i.e., sounded just a fraction of a moment longer—than other staccato quarter notes in the left hand, hence the added bar accent (lunga).

ALTERNATE TAKES, DIFFERENT INSTRUMENTATION

3. WAITING AT THE END OF THE ROAD

Music. Irving Berlin
Lyrics. Irving Berlin
Copyright. E pub. 6663 (10 June 1929)

In Waller's early years at Victor (1927 and 1929), it was the rule in a session, rather than the exception, to record two and occasionally three takes of an individual tune. But Waller recorded "Waiting at the End of the Road" no fewer than four times on 29 August 1929—two takes on piano and two takes on the Camden studio's Estey pipe organ. Of these four, the first take of the piano solo was issued.[1] In only one other instance in Waller's career did the number of takes of a single tune recorded at one session exceed three, and that occurred at this same session—five takes were made of "Baby, Oh Where Can You Be," two on piano and three on organ.[2] While a number of factors could force additional takes, the significant amount of recording time devoted to these two tunes suggests either how popular the Victor producer thought they would prove to be (hence worth the extra effort required to record multiple takes), or how much Waller enjoyed playing them—and perhaps, too, how much he wanted to perform them on pipe organ.

The two performances of "Waiting at the End of the Road" transcribed here, because they were recorded at the same session, provide an especially focused opportunity to contrast Waller's approaches to performance on piano and pipe organ. Waller understood the piano intuitively and technically as a percussive as well as a melodic instrument. He exploited the piano's percussive qualities, particularly through techniques of attack and pedaling, to create a variety of expressive effects and to develop the powerful swing that propels his performances. On piano, Waller could also parade his formidable store of right hand tricks to embellish the melody. Compare, for example, the first A phrase of the chorus in both versions (mm. 21–28, especially mm. 27–28).

The organ, on the other hand, afforded Waller greater improvisational possibilities with timbre, as he could make use of a wide palette of instrumental colors through different registral combinations. In addition, the organ's capability for sudden, dramatic shifts in dynamic level and for a broad range of dynamic contrast in general significantly

---

[1]The second take is transcribed in this volume.

[2]It may be worth noting that the two tunes share a remarkably similar rhythmic profile for the melodic line to which the words of the title are set. Furthermore, Waller's organ versions of "Baby, Oh Where Can You Be" adhere to an interpretative design similar to that of "Waiting at the End of the Road," probably since they were recorded consecutively at the same session.

exceeds that of the piano. Waller took full advantage of both these capabilities for expressive purposes. Indeed, because the organ version of "Waiting at the End of the Road" proceeds at a considerably slower tempo than the piano version, Waller offers what might be described as a more soulful interpretation of the tune (see mm. 5–8 in both versions or either pair of bridge phrases: mm. 37–44 in both versions and mm. 69–76 in the piano version against mm. 71–78 in the organ version). This is not to suggest that Waller avoided uptempo swing on the organ; the final chorus (mm. 55–86) demonstrates conclusively that, as in both versions of "Rusty Pail," Waller's sharp, staccato attack on the manual, and the combination of pedal board notes and left hand chords to simulate a stride bass pattern, constitute an effective method for reproducing the swinging effects of the pianistic stride bass on the organ.

3a. WAITING AT THE END OF THE ROAD

Recorded 29 August 1929 (mx. 55375-2)

Words and Music by
Irving Berlin
as performed by Thomas "Fats" Waller

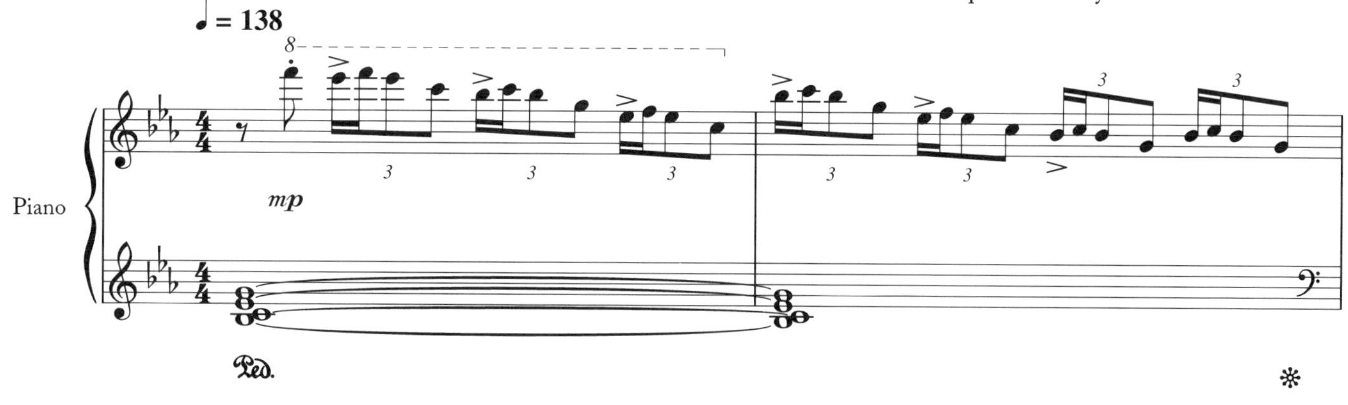

15
18
22
25
28

mf
ossia

Ped.
senza Ped.
p
mp
(8)
8
3

63
(8)
66
69
72
75
5
3
3
Ped.
*

78
Ped.

81
cresc.
mf
Ped.

84
f
Ped.

87
p
Ped.
senza Ped.

90
mf
Ped.

93
(8)
senza Ped.
96
(8)
Ped.
99
(8)
Ped.
102
(8)
Ped.
105
(8)
Ped.

(8)
108
111
(8)
dim.
114
(8)
p
pp

Commentary

Title. Waiting at the End of the Road
Source. Victor 78 rpm master
Matrix number. 55375-2 (unissued)
Recording date. 29 August 1929
Reissue. "Fats" Waller, "Complete Recordings," vol. 4 (RCA 741.086, May 1973, LP)

Performance notes. Both takes of the piano solo share the same structure: a four measure introduction, two eight measure phrases of the verse (mm. 5–12 and mm. 13–20), and three AABA choruses (mm. 21–52, 53–84, and 85–116; a key change from E♭ major to G major occurs in m. 84, the last measure of the second chorus). Both takes also manifest a variation procedure for the second chorus that Waller frequently employs in these early solo piano recordings—transposing the register of the right hand up an octave. The pitches at these higher frequencies seem to have retained greater clarity and a truer timbre in the recording process than their lower counterparts, thus lending an exceptionally clear, bell-like quality to these passages.

As with other takes from these early sessions, Waller's final chorus for the piano takes of "Waiting at the End of the Road" provides a rousing conclusion by outlining the melody in heavily accented chords with dense pitch clusters in the right hand—probably alluding to the "stomp-off" style he would have used at rent parties. Indeed, the second piano take is clearly a somewhat modified version of the first, differing from it only in details of ornamentation, a few harmonic progressions, and the concluding measures, which bring the piece to a close gradually. The closing passage in the second take is both more delicate and more subtle than its counterpart in the first take. Both takes proceed at an almost identical tempo; usually in the early sessions for Victor, where two takes of a performance were made consecutively, the second tended to be faster. The tempo of the second take begins at a pace of quarter note at 138 beats per minute (bpm) but speeds up slightly to about 141 by the second chorus, remaining at that speed until the end, where it slows to 138 again.

An examination of Waller's approach to articulation in the left hand reveals the principal means by which he creates the extraordinarily powerful swing characteristic of his performances. That articulation consists of several crucial components—accent, broken or rolled chords and tenths, judicious use of the damper pedal (in which both depressing the pedal to sustain the sound and suddenly releasing it to stop the sound play an important role), and the mix of sustained and staccato touch. Measures 38–41 provide a glimpse of the basic configuration of these components; however, Waller frequently resorts to a simpler pattern consisting of sharp, staccato chords on each of the four beats of a measure (see mm. 53–56). Waller also consistently accents the top pitch of the chords on the strong beats in the left hand, thereby creating a line that seems to function as a countermelody to the material in the right hand. This line usually descends by steps and extends either over several measures (see mm. 37–41, 57–60, and 69–71) or over a few beats (mm. 51–53). In some instances, even though the constituent pitches may be separated by a beat, the descent takes on the character of an appoggiatura (e.g., the b♭ of m. 31, beat 3 to the a♭ of m. 32, beat 1 and the c♭′ of m. 32, beat 3 to the b♭ of m. 33, beat 1).

Critical notes. M. 4, RH: the pattern of the offbeat b♭′ pitches in the top voice adheres to the normal swung rhythmic profile of eighth notes;

m. 56, beats 1 and 3: Waller may have pedaled lightly on these beats;

m. 66, beat 3, LH: the a♭ is stressed as a step in a descending melodic gesture (a–a♭–g) that extends from m. 66, beat 1 to m. 67, beat 1;

m. 87, beat 1, RH: the grace note may have been intended by Waller as a way of coloring the open octave on the downbeat, but it may also have been a mistake;

m. 100, beats 3 and 4: while not played staccato, the quarter notes on these beats are detached, in contrast to the quarter notes on the first two beats, which are linked; Waller thus provides a greater rhythmic impetus to the beginning of the bridge;

mm. 113–14: Waller may have enhanced the legato articulation of this figure with discreet pedaling.

3b. WAITING AT THE END OF THE ROAD

Recorded 29 August 1929 (mx. 56067-1)

Words and Music by
Irving Berlin
as performed by Thomas "Fats" Waller

13
pp
p
mf
18
rit.
more strictly, ♩ = 104
mp
22
3
26
mf

31
35
mf
40
3
44
ten.
ten.
a tempo (♩ = 104)
mf sub. p
mf
3

ten.
rit.
♩ = 93
ossia
rit.
cresc.
𝆗 = ca. 78
f
mf

(8)
sub. pp
cresc.
mf

meno mosso ♩ = 125
(8)
♩ = 112
rit.
♩ = 78
sub. p
f

Commentary

Title. Waiting at the End of the Road
Source. Victor 78 rpm master
Matrix number. 56067-1 (unissued)
Recording date. 29 August 1929
Reissue. "Fats" Waller, "Complete Recordings," vol. 4 (RCA 741.086, May 1973, LP)

Performance notes. As with the two piano takes, both organ takes follow the same scheme: introduction (mm. 1–4), two verse phrases (mm. 5–12 and mm. 13–20), AABA, thirty-two-measure chorus (mm. 21–51), transition from E♭ major to G major (mm. 52–54), AABA chorus (mm. 55–86). Waller's registration features tremolo prominently throughout, and he selects a particularly florid combination of stops for the introduction and verse phrases. He also seems to rely principally on solo stops (or combinations of stops) to create the focused and penetrating sound characteristic of the right-hand melodic line in the chorus. This quality, coupled with the organ's capability to sustain pitches for unlimited duration, gives the melodic lines on organ their peculiarly vocal essence. The organ's ability to imitate the breath control of the voice and other wind instruments is one of its central attributes that Waller must have found particularly appealing in aesthetic terms. The shutter pedal for the swell organ probably controls the continuous fluctuations in dynamic level in the introduction and verse phrases.

The musical function of each hand on the manuals and the feet on the pedal board is straightforward and fixed throughout the performance. The right hand (probably on the manual for the Solo organ) outlines the melody in single pitches. Exceptions occur at the ends of phrases or in cadential passages (where Waller tends to use chords) and in the final chorus (where Waller's staccato articulation of three- and four-voiced chords in the right hand emphasizes the syncopation inherent in the profile of the melodic line). This denser texture also assists in creating a loud, rich sound appropriate to a stomp-off chorus. The left hand (probably on the Great manual) outlines the harmony by articulating chords on each beat, except for four brief melodic flourishes in the verse phrases. The pedals supply the fundamental note of the harmony, either on the strong beats of the measure or on all four beats.

Critical notes. M. 1, beat 2, RH: the grace note is articulated before the beat and in the context of a swung eighth note pattern;

mm. 11–12; 16; LH: the melodic gesture in the left hand is prominent; Waller must have achieved this stratification either through a change in registration (perhaps by use of couplers) or by shifting manuals;

m. 23, beat 4, RH: the eighth note equals in duration the first two eighth notes of a triplet, and the sixteenth note duplet equals in duration the third eighth note of a triplet (see Apparatus); similar gestures occur at m. 31, beat 4, RH and m. 47, beat 4, RH;

m. 39, beat 2; m. 40, beat 1; m. 41, beat 1, RH: the eighth note equals in duration the first two eighth notes of a triplet, and the sixteenth note duplet equals in duration the third eighth note of a triplet; Waller maintains a clear distinction in the articulation of this gesture and the somewhat similar gesture using grace notes noted in mm. 38 and 39;

m. 45, beat 1, RH: the triplet grace note is articulated before the beat;

mm. 51–53, beats 1–2, RH: the eighth notes are not precisely even, but are nevertheless closer to even articulation than to swung articulation;

m. 70, beat 3, RH: the subito pianissimo, occurring precisely on beat 3, is probably created by closing the swell box;

m. 78, beat 3, RH: the grace note f♯‴ is struck almost simultaneously with the quarter note g‴ and released.

4. I CAN'T GIVE YOU ANYTHING BUT LOVE

Music. Jimmy McHugh
Lyrics. Dorothy Fields
Copyright. E 687442 (6 March 1928)

It is possible that "I Can't Give You Anything But Love," though copyrighted by Fields and McHugh, was actually written by Waller and Razaf.[1] Both takes transcribed here were recorded at the same session, and the arrangement is for Waller's small "Rhythm" group: trumpet (John Hamilton; first take only), tenor saxophone (Gene Sedric), guitar (John Smith), bass (Cedric Wallace), drum set (Slick Jones), piano (Fats Waller), and voice (Waller sings both takes, while Una Mae Carlisle, a former Waller protégée, sings only on take one).[2] Nevertheless, the two takes project fundamentally different interpretations of the lyrics by Waller (see Introduction: Verbal Dueling, for a discussion of the performance recorded on take one). For the vocal solo of take two, Waller replaces the verbal aggression of the first take with a more gentle, solicitous stance—though as in the first take, he interpolates text frequently and richly embellishes the tune. (See Apparatus: Notation—Text, for a description of the symbols used in the vocal transcription.)

Transcription note. In both takes, the sound quality of the recording is such that the pitches of the piano, the solo instruments, and the bass are occasionally obscured, as is Waller's use of the damper pedal.

---

[1]See Barry Singer, *Black and Blue: The Life and Lyrics of Andy Razaf* (New York: Schirmer Books, 1992), 210–11 and Paul S. Machlin, "Fats Waller Composes: The Sketches, Drafts, and Lead Sheets in the Institute of Jazz Studies Collection," *Annual Review of Jazz Studies (1994–1995)* (Lanham, Md., and London: Scarecrow Press, 1996), 2.

[2]The entry in Brian Rust's discography *Jazz Records 1897–1942* (p. 1635) in this regard is incorrect.

4a. I CAN'T GIVE YOU ANYTHING BUT LOVE

Recorded 3 November 1939 (mx. 043351-1)

Words by
Dorothy Fields

Music by Jimmy McHugh
as performed by Fats Waller and His Rhythm
Una Mae Carlisle and Thomas "Fats" Waller, voice

T. Sax
Gtr.
B.
Dr.
Pn.
p
A♭6
A♭6
[brushes, stirring]
simile
CARLISLE
mp
I can't give you an - y - thing but love,
Ped.
E♭7
E♭7
A♭6
Ba - by.
That's the on - ly thing

T. Sax
Gtr.
B.
Pn.
WALLER
A♭6
E♭7
E♭7
I've plen - ty of, oh, Ba - by.
Don't you tell me; yes, what am I sup-posed
A♭7
A♭7
D♭6
Dream a - while, scheme a - while, you're sure to
to do? Yes. You're wrong.

16
D♭6
B7
B♭7
B♭7
find
hap - pi - ness,
and I guess,
That's what you think I'm sure to find.
{Um hmm}
19
E♭7
E♭°
E♭7
A♭6
all those things you're sure to pine for.
Gee, I'd love to see

22
A♭6
[F7]
B♭min7
you
look - in' swell,
mp
Well my tai - lor's wait - in' right out - side the
24
E♭7
A♭7
Ba - by,
Dia - mond brace - lets
door, [He can] keep me look - in' swell, I ain't [play - in']

Ab7
Db6
Wool-worth's does - n't sell, my lit-tle
mp
I nev-er had a dia-mond brace-
Db6
Db6
Ba - by.
'Til that luck-y day,
let in my life; what do I want it for?

30
D♭min6
A♭
F7
you know darn well,
ooo,
Ba - by, that I
5
What hap-pens? What goes on in here?
33
Saxophone tacet to end (mm. 36–69)
B♭min7
E♭7
A♭6
Carlisle tacet to end (mm. 36–69)
mp
can't give you an - y - thing but love.
3
mp

36
Trumpet (cup mute)
Tpt.
Gtr.
B.
Pn.
p
B♭min7
E♭7
A♭6
C♭°
mp
mf
Come here, let me tell you some-thin':
{I} can't dish out an - y - thing but love,
39
B♭min7
E♭7
B♭min7
E♭7
A♭6
E♭7
f
{Ba'!}
{That's} the {on} - ly thing

42
A♭6
B°
E♭7
E♭9
E♭7
f
mf
{I've got} plen - ty {of,}
{Ba - by.}
45
A♭7
A♭7
mp
f
You talk - in' 'bout dream - in' a - while,
{schem - in' a - while,}

mp
you're sure to find
D♭6
B7
B♭7
mf
hap - pi - ness,
pp
and I guess,

51
E♭7
E♭7
E♭[9]
E♭7
mf
all ___ those fine A - ra - bi - an things your lit - tle heart pines for, yes.
53
A♭6
A♭6
C♭°
mp
Skip 'em!
I'd love to see you

55
E♭7
F°
E♭9
E♭7
look - in' swell.
57
A♭7
A♭7
A♭9/7
{Dia - mond brace - lets?}
Wool - worth ain't got no busi - ness sell-in' 'em;

59
D♭6
D♭6
A♭7
mp
mf
you can go to, go (t') ah, well, ah well, well, well. Ho,
61
D♭6
D♭min6
A♭6
f
'til that luck - y day, you know {darn} well, well,

64
F7
B♭min7
E♭9
E♭7
Ba - by, I ain't dish - in' out no - thin', ain't get - tin' {off} on {noth - in'} __ {but love.}
67
rit.
Tpt.
A♭
Gtr.
B.
Dr.
p
How's that, Babes? There's your dia-monds.
Pn.

Commentary

Title. I Can't Give You Anything But Love
Source. Victor 78 rpm
Matrix number. 043351-1
Recording date. 3 November 1939
Reissue. "Fats" Waller and His Rhythm, Complete Recordings (1939), vol. 18 (RCA FXM1 7316, 1976, LP)

Performance notes. There is a remarkable contrast in style between the melodic lines crafted by Sedric on saxophone to accompany Carlisle's vocal and Hamilton's on trumpet to accompany Waller. Each instrumentalist cannily mirrors each singer: Sedric's large note values and conjunct motion provide an organic counterpart to Carlisle's smooth lines and elegant phrasing, while Hamilton's more florid line with its profusion of triplet figures reflects the increased rhythmic activity of Waller's performance, though not its more erratic rhythmic values and shorter, choppier phrases. Carlisle's timbre is rich and throaty, with a fast and tight vibrato apparent on extended pitches; her interpretation of the song is simple, direct, and understated. Her legato is facilitated by almost constant use of portamento, and she has a tendency to close early to final voiced consonants, particularly "ng," "l," and "nt."

Critical notes. M. 15, beat 3; m. 16, beat 1; Carlisle: the sixteenth-note embellishments are substantial enough to be rendered as pitches with rhythmic value, as opposed to grace notes (see Carlisle, m. 13 and m. 32);

m. 16, beat 1: Waller begins the phrase with a brief chuckle;

m. 24, beat 1: the first syllable of Carlisle's "baby" ends abruptly with a closed "b"; thus, there is a clear if momentary interruption in the vocal sound between the two syllables of the word "baby";

m. 24, beat 4: Waller's verb ("playin' ") may also be understood as a contraction of "complaining" (that is, " 'plainin' ").

4b. I CAN'T GIVE YOU ANYTHING BUT LOVE

Recorded 3 November 1939 (mx. 043351-2)

Words by
Dorothy Fields

Music by Jimmy McHugh
as performed by Thomas "Fats" Waller and His Rhythm
Thomas "Fats" Waller, voice

7
B.
Pn.
8
9
12

15
mp
18
8
9
p
20
(8)
9
mp
22

25
28
31
34
dim.
p
mp
pp

37
T. Sax
Gtr.
B.
Ab6
Eb7
WALLER
I can't give you an - y - thing but love,
Pn.
40
Eb7
Ab6
Ba-by,
That's the on - ly {fine} thing

42
A♭6
E♭7
E♭7
I've got plen-ty of,
{Ba-by,}
you {can} go
45
A♭7
A♭7
mf
and {dream} a - while,
{you can} steam a - while and {scheme} a - while,

D♭6
D♭
C♭7
B♭7
mp
You're {bound} to {find} ___
{Hap}-pi - ness,
B♭7
E♭9
E♭°
E♭7
mf
f
{And} I guess, ___
{all} those {things} your {heart} al - ways pines for.

53
A♭6
A♭6
mp
Gee, {I'd l - ove} to {see} you look - in' swell,

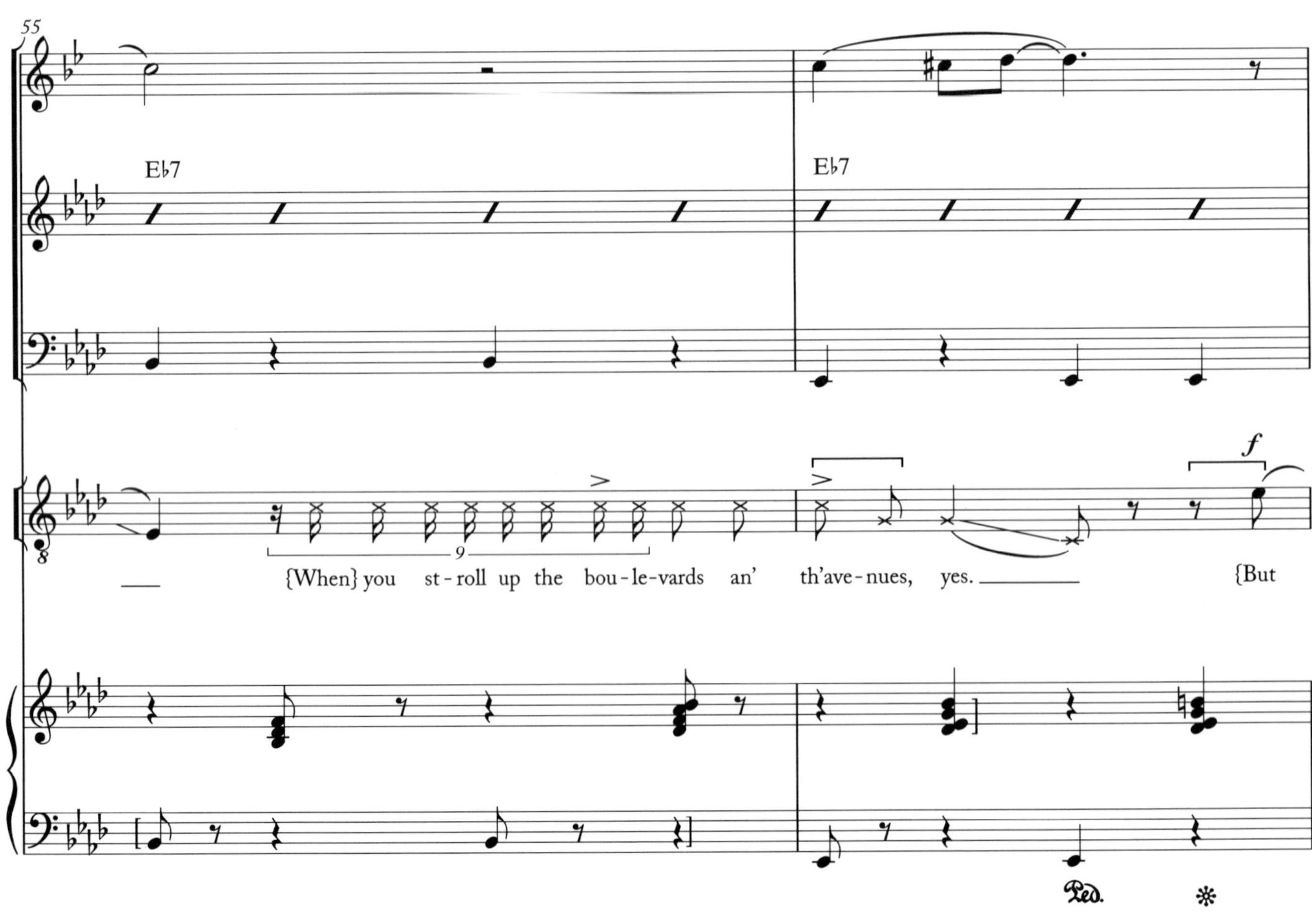
55
E♭7
E♭7
f
{When} you st - roll up the bou - le - vards an' th'ave - nues, yes. {But

57
A♭7
A♭7
mp
dia} - mond brace - {lets,}
{Dah,}
That cat known as {Wool}-worth
5
59
D♭6
D♭6
A♭7
3
don't sell 'em,
No,
Nev-er heard
of him!

61
D♭6
D♭min6
mp
'Til that luck - y day,
I might hit the num-bers to-mor-row,
63
A♭
E♭min6
F7
Ba - by, If I do you gon - na look darn swell, Ba - by,

65
B♭min7
E♭9/7
E♭7
But for the time be-in', for the pre-sent, Wel-come to the fu-ture, I can't give you an - y-thing but
67
T. Sax
Gtr.
B.
Dr.
Pn.
A♭6
E♭7
A♭6
love.
senza rit.
8
Ped.
Ped.
Ped.

Commentary

Title. I Can't Give You Anything But Love
Source. Victor 78 rpm
Matrix number. 043351-2 (unissued)
Recording date. 3 November 1939
Reissue. "Fats" Waller and His Rhythm, Complete Recordings (1939), vol. 18 (RCA FXM1 7316, 1976, LP)

Critical notes. M. 13, beat 2–m. 16, beat 4, piano: this passage is probably played with the left hand crossing over the right on beats two and four in order to articulate the chords above the melodic line;

m. 17, beat 4, RH: the grace notes are played with the g″; the initial b♭″ grace note is tied to the final eighth note b♭″;

m. 26, beats 1 and 4; m. 27, beat 1; RH: each of the initial grace notes on these three beats may be tied to the quarter note it embellishes;

m. 37 ff.: Gene Sedric on tenor saxophone basically recapitulates the melody, rather than improvising a new line, so that Waller's intricate and rhythmically complex line is heard against a spare rendition of the original;

m. 60, beat 4, tenor sax: though the sound of the pitch e♭″ (notated as f″) in this range is present on the recording, it is possible that it is the result of a harmonic on the piano rather than a separate pitch articulated by the tenor sax.

DIFFERENT SESSIONS, SAME INSTRUMENTATION

5. I'M CRAZY 'BOUT MY BABY

Music. Thomas "Fats" Waller
Lyrics. Alexander Hill
Copyright. EU34757 (14 February 1931)

Waller originally recorded "I'm Crazy 'Bout My Baby" with Ted Lewis and His Band on 6 March 1931—it was the first time his singing voice was captured on a recording. The comparison with his solo recording of the song one week later (i.e., this transcription) is instructive. With Lewis's band, Waller sings in a straightforward, occasionally even tentative manner, embellishing the composed melodic line and text only minimally and avoiding modifications to his vocal timbre. In his own recording, however, he takes many liberties—improvising, signifying on text and music, and generally advancing a biting satiric agenda. By the time of the Muzak recording, almost exactly four years later, Waller had mastered the use of verbal play, particularly in terms of text alteration, vocal timbre modification, and rhythmic and pitch manipulation. Nevertheless, the text of Waller's opening monologue in the Muzak performance is clearly derived, if somewhat truncated, from the 1931 take. The overall shape of individual sung phrases seems based on the earlier recording as well, though the details differ extensively. In both Waller adopts similar and somewhat tempered performance strategies on the piano: he accompanies the vocal verse and choruses with a skeletal stride pattern, divided between hands and occasionally enriched by a single mid-range pitch (two or four beats in length), and he inserts stride solos between the sung passages (spiced, in the 1931 version, with spoken commentary). He plays the solos in both recordings with comparative restraint, restricting his use of the damper pedal and maintaining a fairly consistent dynamic level. This combination produces a relatively dry, clear timbre. Finally, throughout each version, he outlines the stride bass pattern in a detached but not heavily accented articulation.

The sequence of standard thirty-two-measure choruses (each divided into an AABA phrase scheme) is plotted somewhat differently for each recording (see figure 2), resulting in overall structures of unequal length. This was probably due to the different functions of each session: the 1931 performance was for a commercial 78 rpm recording, while the Muzak performance was part of a medley of three tunes linked together for a transcription disc. Thus, the length and structure of each take was dictated in part by its context.

Mx. 151417-3	**Muzak**
Introduction (mm. 1–8)	Introduction (mm. 1–8)
Verse (mm. 9–24)	Verse (mm. 9–24)
Chorus A—vocal (mm. 24–56)	Chorus A—vocal (mm. 24–56)
Chorus A′—piano (mm. 56–88)	Chorus A′—piano (mm. 56–88)
Chorus A″—vocal (mm. 88–120)	Chorus A″—vocal (mm. 88–120)
Chorus A‴	Coda—vocal (mm. 120–22)
piano (mm. 120–36)	
vocal (mm. 136–52)	
Coda—vocal (mm. 152–54)	

FIGURE 2. Comparison of form in two performances of "I'm Crazy 'Bout My Baby"

5a. I'M CRAZY 'BOUT MY BABY

Recorded 13 March 1931 (mx. 151417-3)

Words by
Alexander Hill

Music by
Thomas "Fats" Waller

mf
walk-in', walk-in' on air,
for I've left all my
mf
mp
b(uh)-lue days be - hind,
Oh ba - by,
I've
learned how to care,
And there's love, real - ly
love, on my mind.
I'm the {world's} most hap-py crea -

26
sub. p
- ture, {Tell} me, {what} can wor - ry be? I'm cra - zy 'bout my ba -
30
mp
by, And m' ba - by's cra - zy 'bout me. Mis - ter
33
sub. p
Cu - pid was the teach - er, That's the rea - son we a - {gree.} I'm
37
mf
cra - zy 'bout my ba - by, And m' ba - by's cra - zy 'bout

p
me. Par - son, get that book out, read - y in your
mp
ha - nd. Keep a stead - y look - out,
cresc.
mf
You can un - der - st - a - nd: It's an A – One com - bin - a -
mp
- tion with the per - fect he and sh - e I'm cra - zy 'bout m' ba -

(gradual accel. to m. 73)
mf
by, And my ba-by's cra-zy 'bout me.
mp
mf
Let's waltz the rum-ba!
𝅗𝅥 = 98
{Boy,} will you get off?

66
69
Now let's go up -
72
town, uh.
𝅗𝅥 = 100
Oh, we're now
75
float - in' down the Hud - son, mer - cy, oh, you sl - ay me, you

78
sweet thing,
oh,
ba - by, eh!
(8)
3
cresc.
81
mf
84
87
𝅗𝅥 = 96
mf
{Oh, I'm} the world's most hap - (py) crea - ture,
p
3

91
Tell me, what can w-or - ry be? I'm cra - zy 'bout m' ba -
94
mp
mf
by, And m' ba-by's cra-zy 'bout me. Oh, Mis - ter Cu-pid was
3
98
3
sub. p
the teach-er, Oh, the rea - son we a - gree. I'm so
101
3
cra - zy a - bout my ba - by hmm, my ba - by's cra - zy 'bout

104
pp
p
me. Par - son, get that book out, Get that book out and hold it stead - y,
107
p
Hold it stead-y in your hand. Keep a stead - y look - out,
110
cresc.
f
sure - ly you can, sure - ly you can {un} - der - stand. It's an
113
A – One com - bin - a - tion, mmm The per-fect he and sh-e,

117
Oh, I'm cra - zy 'bout my ba - by,
And my ba - by's cra - zy
120
accel.
♩ = 100
'bout me.
mf
senza Ped.
123
126

129
(8)
Ped.
132
(8)
3
Ped.
135
mf
Oh Par - son, get th'
Ped.
senza Ped.
138
f
book out, hold it stead-y in {your} hand, Keep stead-y l -

142
-ook {out,} you can un - der - st - and. {It's} an
145
A – {One} com - bin - a - {tion,} oh th' per - fect he and sh - e,
149
I'm ex - as - per - a - ted 'bout my off - spring, my off - spring's ex - as - per - a - ted 'bout
rit.
mf
p
152
rubato
me. Now lis - ten would you like to come o - ver for a cup of coff - ee, mm' Ba - by? May - be.
ten.
ten.

Commentary

Title. I'm Crazy 'Bout My Baby
Source. Columbia 78 rpm
Matrix number. 151417-3
Recording date. 13 March 1931
Reissue. "Fats" Waller Plays, Sings, Alone and with Various Groups (CBS 63366 [France], n.d., LP)

Performance notes. For a detailed account of this recording, in particular of Waller's rendition of the text and the spoken interpolations, see Paul S. Machlin, *Stride*, 34–40.

Critical notes. M. 2 ff.: it is possible that Waller uses the damper pedal discreetly on beats 1 and 3 throughout the spoken monologue;

m. 42, beat 3; m. 44, beats 3–4; RH: passages such as these in which the right hand doubles the vocal line are unusual in Waller's performances;

m. 53, beat 2, voice: the long "e" vowel in "crazy" is cut off early by a combination of a glottal stop and the formation of the consonant "b" in preparation for the next word—"baby";

m. 59, beat 3, RH: the triple pitch grace note is articulated almost simultaneously with the fourth pitch of the subsequent chord, c‴;

m. 60, beat 1, RH: although the b♭″ is notated as a whole note, the performer will have to release it just before the last eighth note of the measure in order to play the final dyad, which also contains the pitch b♭″;

m. 65, beats 1–2, voice: the phrase "get off" may (1) refer to a "get-off," or flashy, pianist; (2) suggest intense involvement with, or enjoyment of, the act of playing (as in "getting off" on playing); or (3) be an invitation to vacate the piano stool so the next stride player (Waller?) can take over;

mm. 70–71, LH: Waller articulates the eight quarter notes of these two measures clearly in a 3 + 3 + 2 grouping, as opposed to the 4 + 4 grouping of the right hand (see also mm. 86–87, 126–27, and 134–35);

m. 90, beat 2, voice: Waller cuts off the vowel of the second syllable of the word "happy";

m. 112, beat 1, voice: the downbeat falls on the second of the two grace notes, i.e., the grace note g′ is articulated simultaneously with the left hand BB♭;

m. 131, beat 4, RH: the grace note on the second eighth note is played simultaneously with the octave.

5b. I'M CRAZY 'BOUT MY BABY

Recorded 11 March 1935
(Muzak Transcription Disk A-267)

Words by
Alexander Hill

Music by
Thomas "Fats" Waller

14
mf
b(uh)-lue {days} be - hi - nd. I've
18
mp
learned how to {care} yes, yes, And there's lo - ve, real - ly love,
22
rit.
a tempo 𝅗𝅥 = ca. 112
mf
on my mind. {I'm} the {world's} most hap - py crea-
rit.
a tempo
mp
26
mp
- ture, Tell me, what can wor - ry be? I'm cra - zy 'bout my

30
mf
ba - by,
Ba - by's cra - zy 'bout me.
Mis - ter {Cu} - pid was the teach-
34
- er,
3
{and} the rea - son {we} a - gree.
{I'm
37
cra - zy 'bout m'} ba - by,
Ba - by's cra - zy 'bout me.
p
Par - son,
41
1/4 tone
get that book,
Hold it in your hand.
mp
Keep a stead-y

45
mf
l - ook - out,
You can {un - der - stand:}
It's an
49
{A - one} com - bin - a - tion,
Per-fect {he and she.}
I'm
53
f
cra - zy 'bout {my} ba - by,
{Ba}-by's cra - zy 'bout me.
57
senza Ped.
60
3

63
f
[Ped. ❊]
66
[Ped. ❊ Ped. ❊]
69
72
mf
[Ped. ❊]
Ped. ❊
75
†
Ped. ❊
78
mp
mf
Ped. ❊ [Ped. ❊ Ped. ❊]
Ped.
†

81
84
Ped.
87
mf
{I'm} the {world's} most {ha} - p' crea - ture,
mp
91
Tell me, wha' can w - or - ry be?
Cra - zy {'bout my
94
mp
ba - by,}
Ba - by's cra - zy 'bout me.

97
mf
{Cu}-pid {was} the teach - er,
And the rea - son
[Ped. ❊]
100
we a - gree. I'm cra - zy {'bout my} ba - by,
Ped. ❊
103
mp cresc.
Ba-{by's cra} - zy 'bout me. {Par - son, get that book, Hold it in
107
mf
your hand,} Keep a stead-y {l - ook} - out {you can
[Ped. ❊
Ped. ❊]

111
un - der - st - and.} {It's an A - one com - bin - a} - tion, A
115
mf
per - {fect he and she,} I'm ex - as - p' - ra - ted {'bout} the off - spring, and the
119
rit.
off - spring's 'sas - p' - rat - ed {'bout} me. Yes, yes, yes. Uh oh,
122
look - a here, Here she is now; come on in, hon - ey; yeah, let's sit down . . .

Commentary

Title. I'm Crazy 'Bout My Baby

Source. Muzak-Associated 16-inch transcription disc; with "Tea for Two" and "Believe It, Beloved"

Program / Disc number. A-267

Recording date. 11 March 1935

Reissues. "Fats" Waller (Hitherto Unpublished Piano, Vocal and Conversation), vol. 1 (RCA 730.659, n.d. [ca. 1972–1973], LP) and "Oh Mercy! Looka' Here" Fats Waller, His Piano, His Rhythm—1935 & 1939 (HSR 5000-1, 1981, LP)

Performance notes. The performance for Muzak proceeds at a faster tempo and is, in many respects, more concise than its 1931 counterpart. Waller breaks his momentum only briefly at the end of the verse. In the first of the three choruses that follow, he uses, in each of the three A phrases, a noticeably exaggerated timbre and pronunciation for the title line of text, as opposed to the standard vocal quality for the antecedent half-phrase. This heightened contrast between the two segments of text in each phrase serves both to emphasize the title of the song and to signify on it. The satiric nature of the vocal timbre and pronunciation suggest that the real nature of the relationship may be much less affectionate than that implied by the title line.

The second chorus consists of a piano solo without any interpolation of text, as distinct from the 1931 recording. As in other of Waller's solo work (e.g., "Honeysuckle Rose, à la Bach, Beethoven, Brahms, and Waller")—but in complete contrast to the 1931 recording—the bridge is based on a single motivic idea altered to fit the changing harmony on every other beat. In the third chorus, Waller reverses the strategy employed in the first: that is, he reworks the first half of each phrase extensively in terms of the melodic line (and, to a lesser extent, the pronunciation), but simplifies his singing of the title line. In addition, the right hand of the piano doubles (while embellishing) the vocal line for these two phrases—this is an unusual texture for Waller's vocal passages. The beginning of the vocal line for the bridge (mm. 104–6) is reminiscent of the final statement of this line in the 1931 recording (mm. 137–40). For the final A phrase, however, Waller returns to the spoken voice he employed for the introduction, and (as in the 1931 recording) makes explicit the signified meaning implied in his invocation of the title line in the first chorus ("I'm exasperated 'bout the offspring . . ."). Legato phrasing in the voice is indicated in the transcription by slur lines; where these are absent, Waller uses a percussive articulation in his voice.

Critical notes. M. 9: Waller picks up the tempo here almost imperceptibly;

mm. 23–24: in contrast to the unbroken pace of the 1931 version, Waller here creates a clear structural division between the verse and the chorus by using a significant ritard; the change of meter in the transcription is intended only to reflect the rhythm as Waller plays it rather than his conception of the meter itself;

m. 102, beat 3, LH: the grace note is probably a slip of the finger.

6. HONEYSUCKLE ROSE

Music. Thomas "Fats" Waller
Lyrics. Andy Razaf
Copyright. EU10784 (11 September 1929)

In his liner notes to the three-LP boxed set of reissued recordings that Waller had originally recorded for radio broadcast (*"Oh Mercy! Looka' Here" Fats Waller, His Piano, His Rhythm—1935 & 1939*), Dan Morgenstern suggests that Waller "must have played this tune ["Honeysuckle Rose"] every working day of his life, and had a hundred ways of doing it." Although the two performances transcribed here share an atmosphere of whimsy, they are, in almost all other respects, entirely distinct conceptions (see Introduction: Parody, as well as Performance Notes for Transcription 6 below).

6a. HONEYSUCKLE ROSE

Recorded 11 March 1935

(Muzak Transcription Disk A-268)

Words by
Andy Razaf

Music by
Thomas "Fats" Waller

12
p
Ped.
14
16
18
3
5
21
pp
cresc.
mp
pp

mp
pp
mp
cresc.
mf
dim.

8
pp
(8)
mp
mf
sub. pp

senza cresc.
mp
mp

62
dim.
pp
8
64
65
rit.
67
8

Commentary

Title. Honeysuckle Rose

Source. Muzak-Associated 16-inch Transcription Disc; with "Sweet Sue" and "Somebody Stole My Gal"

Program / Disc number. A-268

Recording date. 11 March 1935

Reissue. "Fats" Waller (Hitherto Unpublished Piano, Vocal and Conversation), vol. 2 (RCA 730.660, February 1973, LP) and "Oh Mercy! Looka' Here" Fats Waller, His Piano, His Rhythm—1935 & 1939 (HSR 5000-1, 1981, LP)

Performance notes. This performance constitutes an example of the subdued and understated—yet marvelously elegant—style of playing that would appear with increasing frequency in Waller's output towards the end of his life. It consists of a four-measure introduction followed by a pair of thirty-two-measure AABA choruses. Each of the total of six A phrases is unique in terms of melodic shape and embellishment, but those of the second chorus are more radically varied, bearing only a tenuous relationship to the original profile of the tune.

Waller maintains a remarkably steady tempo throughout (quarter note at 93 bpm), almost unwavering from beginning to end, and varies his dynamic level only within a very narrow range. Basically, the performance fluctuates delicately between pianissimo and mezzo-piano. (Indeed, there are only four gestures in the entire recording for which Waller plays at a mezzo-forte level [mm. 34, 45, 47, and 48].) It is as if he chooses to restrict these two basic performance parameters in order to focus his creative energies exclusively on the melodic line, embellishing it through the use of a wide assortment of stride tricks, while also substituting new licks that completely obscure the original melodic shape. Nevertheless, despite the unvarying tempo and restricted dynamic range, a sense of rhapsody envelops this performance, created by Waller's delicacy of touch, variety and placement of accents, unexpected shifts in articulation from silky legato to sharp staccato, and asymmetric phrase lengths. Waller's pedaling, however, remains something of an intractable issue here. Normally, at this tempo and in a performance of this subtlety, one would expect Waller to pedal on the first and third beats of each measure, unless chord changes occurred on each beat (e.g., mm. 9, 12, 28, etc.). But due to the age and generally poor fidelity of the recording, it is difficult to establish how much Waller adhered to this formula, and precisely how the pedaling was articulated (especially the release of the damper pedal). In this light, the editor has enclosed in brackets those pedal articulations that could not be established beyond doubt (see Apparatus: Notation—General).

Finally, Waller uses swung eighth notes throughout in both right and left hands, and he articulates all grace notes on the beat with the exceptions cited on the page and confirmed in the specific performance notes.

Critical notes. Mm. 1–2, beat 1, RH: the glissandos are played before the beat;

m. 12, beat 1, RH: the rising chromatic grace note run is articulated before the beat;

m. 13, beat 3, RH: Waller plays this and subsequent configurations metrically (mm. 14–16), as rendered; that is, they are not articulated simply as indeterminate tremolos; it is difficult to determine the extent to which each of these figures is pedaled; the editor suggests the following half-pedaling scheme: mm. 13 and 14, beat 3; m. 15, beats 3 and 4; and m. 16, beat 1;

m. 19, LH: Waller emphasizes the step-wise melodic line in the left hand (eighth notes e′–d′–e′–f′–e′–d′–c′);

m. 20, beats 2–4, RH: the six eighth notes are not articulated exactly as even eighth notes, but nor, on the other hand, are they precisely swung in pairs—Waller's articulation lies between these two;

m. 24, beat 3, RH: the rising chromatic grace-note run is articulated before the beat;

m. 27, beat 2, RH: in this rising chromatic grace-note run the arrival of the second beat can be felt at the articulation of the b♭″, midway through the run;

m. 28, beats 1 and 2, RH: even though the pitches of the figure are repeated exactly, these two gestures are articulated differently, as they appear in the score—that is, beat 1 as a rapid, on-the-beat grace note followed by a pair of swung eighth notes, and beat 2 as an even triplet; it is probable Waller did not intentionally use two different articulations for these two gestures, and, if so, he would not have conceived this difference in notation;

m. 37, beat 1; m. 39, beat 1; RH: swung eighth notes;

m. 41, beat 1; m. 42, beat 3; RH: the a‴ grace note played before the beat in both instances may have been the result of a slip of Waller's finger;

m. 54, beats 1 and 3; m. 55, beat 1; RH: the use of a grace note (tied to the next beat) for the lower pitch of the dyad that begins each of these gestures is intended in the transcription to reflect the rolled articulation Waller uses; because this entire performance is pervaded with a sense of musical caprice, there is no compelling reason to believe that Waller necessarily would have intended each of the right-hand tricks in measures 53–55 and 57–59 to be played in a consistent articulation;

m. 65, beat 3; m. 66, beats 1 and 3; m. 67, beats 1 and 3; RH: the rising chromatic grace-note runs are articulated on the beat, in contrast to previous statements of similar gestures.

6b. HONEYSUCKLE ROSE

à la Bach, Beethoven, Brahms, and Waller

Recorded 13 May 1941 (mx. 063890-1)

Words by
Andy Razaf

Music by
Thomas "Fats" Waller

rit.
sub. p
ten.
mf
mp
meno mosso
a tempo
Ped.
rit.
ten.
8
= 110
= 90
= 110
[ten.]
mp
p
ten.
= 95
rit.
a tempo
p
ten.
= 110
mp

𝅗𝅥 = 99
p
mp
Ped.
swung
rit.
freely, ♩ = ca. 100
even
rit.
mf
a tempo
accel.
rit.
ten.
𝅗𝅥 = ca. 100
swung (RH & LH)
even (RH only)
cresc.

40
rit.
ten.
ten.
†
quasi arpeggio
Ped.
𝅗𝅥 = ca. 76
42
p
swung 16ths
44
simile
simile
46
ossia
48
rit.
even (RH & LH)
mf
†

a tempo
even 16ths
50
simile
rit.
ten.
a tempo
52
rit.
a tempo
𝅗𝅥 = ca. 104
swung (RH & LH)
54
f
even 16ths
𝅘𝅥 = 110
rit.
swung
57
dim.
60
even
𝅘𝅥 = 88
ten.
accel.
swung
mf
f

(8)
62
♩ = 142
even 16ths
ten.
mf
66
swung
70
rit.
even
ten.
♩. = 64
f
♪ = ♪
74
𝅗𝅥 = 64
mf
76
𝅗𝅥 = 78
3
simile

79
mf
cresc.
f

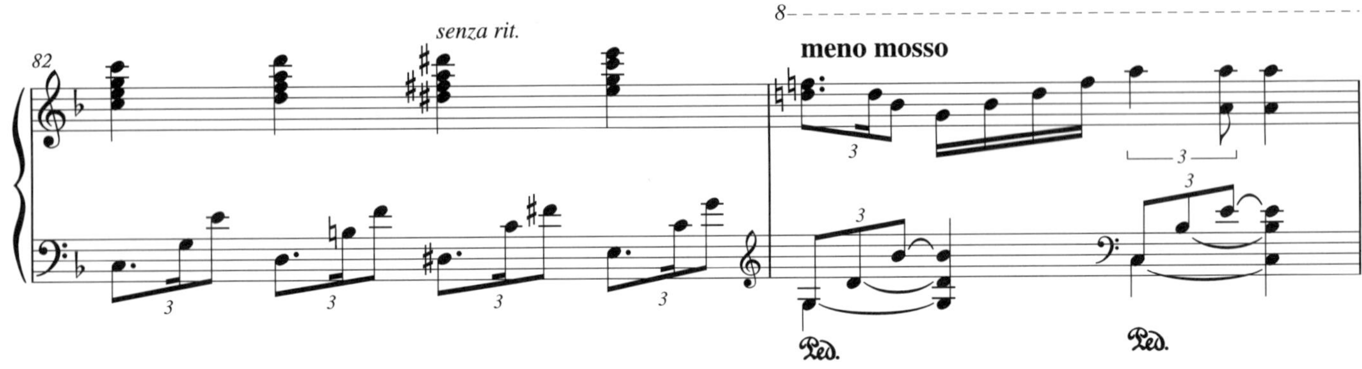
82
senza rit.
8
meno mosso
Ped.
Ped.

(8)
84
a tempo
rit.
dim.
even
Ped.
Ped.
Ped.
Ped.
Ped.

(8)
86
a tempo
accel.
swung (RH & LH)
= 162
mf
f
Ped.
Ped.
senza Ped.

90
simile

94

98

102
♩ = 115
(3)
ff
Ped.
Ped.
Ped.
Ped.
Ped.
Ped.
Ped.
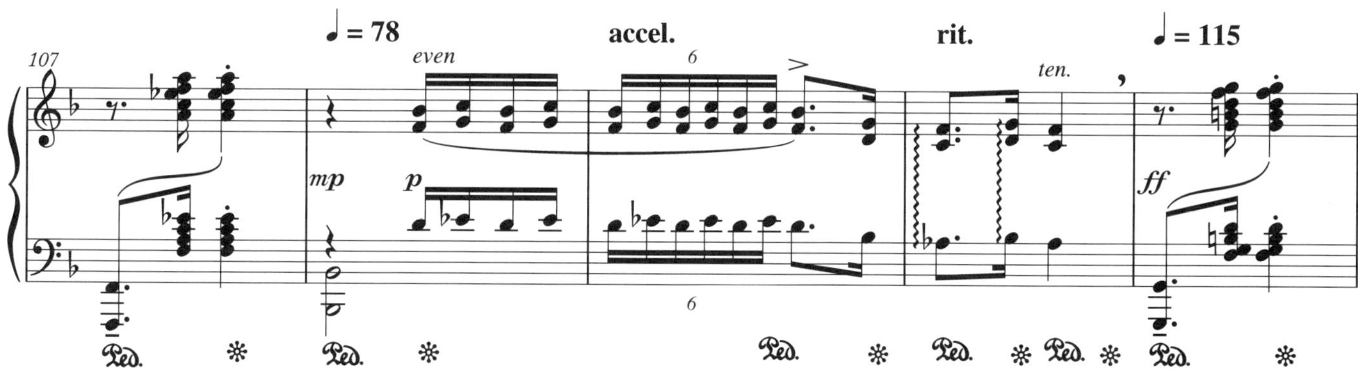
107
♩ = 78
accel.
rit.
♩ = 115
even
6
ten.
mp
p
ff
6
Ped.
Ped.
Ped.
Ped.
Ped.
Ped.

112
accel.
15ma
ff
gliss.
Ped.
Ped.
Ped.
Ped.
Ped.

♩= 88
accel.
swung
8
p
Ped.
rit.
even
ten.
♩= 100
mp
cresc.
simile
ten.
ten.
♩= 115
ff
f
cresc.
simile
8
ff

Commentary

Title. Honeysuckle Rose, à la Bach, Beethoven, Brahms, and Waller
Source. Victor 78 rpm
Matrix number. 063890-1
Recording date. 13 May 1941
Reissue. "Fats" Waller Memorial, vol. 1 (RCA 730.570, 1969, LP) and "Fats" Waller and His Rhythm, Complete Recordings, vol. 22 (1941) (RCA PM 42396, 1978, LP)

Performance notes. Like the previous performance for Muzak-Associated, "Honeysuckle Rose, à la Bach, Beethoven, Brahms, and Waller" is remarkable for its fertility of invention; Waller's playing projects a rhapsodic, whimsical atmosphere, but unlike the earlier recording, he creates this effect through extreme fluctuations in all parameters—particularly tempo, dynamics, and eighth-note articulation.

Waller organizes the performance as an introduction (mm. 1–3), a statement of the verse music (mm. 4–14), and four distinctive variations of the chorus (mm. 15–41, 42–60, 61–88, 89–125; the different lengths of these four choruses reflect Waller's flexible approach to structure in varying his material). The introduction includes gestures borrowed from virtuoso playing in the classical style. Each of three succeeding variations on the chorus represents Waller's take on differing stylistic characteristics of classical music, perhaps as found in the music of the composers cited in the subtitle (see Introduction: Parody). The first two phrases of the fourth concluding variation, however, are pure stride, and must be executed at a dizzying speed until the bridge.

Establishing appropriate tempos for the performance of "Honeysuckle Rose, à la Bach, Beethoven, Brahms, and Waller" is a complex task. The metronome marks indicated in the transcription represent an accurate determination of Waller's speed at the points at which they have been inserted. However, except for the first part of the stride variation (mm. 89–104), Waller imbues the entire rendition with an exceptional amount of rubato. Thus, even within a few beats of the place where a metronome mark appears, the pace of the music may shift abruptly (m. 31, for example). In addition to the variety of metronome speeds noted in the score, the frequency with which such markings as *ritard, tenuto, ad. lib.,* and "freely," are invoked suggest the extent of Waller's interpretive nuance in performance.

In some instances, the most appropriate method for incorporating this flexibility into the score is to alter the meter itself, even though Waller himself almost certainly would not have harbored such a concept. Nonetheless, a shifting metrical structure can, at the appropriate moments, provide a more precise indication of what occurs in Waller's recorded performance—particularly insofar as accentuation of the beat is concerned—than would the invocation of descriptive terms in the score. Similarly, the use of differing rhythmic profiles to outline figures that look (and perhaps even sound on first hearing) as if they are simply repeated is intended to indicate how Waller actually performed the passages in question (see the right hand gestures of m. 51). Also in keeping with the unpredictable nature of the performance, Waller mixes swung and evenly articulated eighth and sixteenth notes. Occasionally, he even uses both simultaneously in different hands (m. 37).

Where the dynamic range of the Muzak disc is limited and subdued, in this version Waller employs the full spectrum of dynamics from *piano* to *fortissimo* (as compared to the same decibel scale as the Muzak performance). These volume changes incorporate near-violent shifts, gradual transitions, and brief passages (usually one measure in length) that Waller repeats as an echo. In addition, because variation was focused on the melodic line and right hand gestures in the Muzak performance, Waller added grace notes frequently as a form of embellishment. In "Honeysuckle Rose, à la Bach, Beethoven, Brahms, and Waller," however, grace notes appear only sparingly and are usually articulated on the beat. Perhaps the scarcity of graces here reflects the abundance of other embellishment strategies as all parameters are subject to significant variation.

Critical notes. M. 1, beat 3, LH: the notation of the tied c″ in the left hand is intended to indicate a continuation of the sonority through use of the pedal while the right hand articulates its descending arpeggio, although technically, of course, it is not possible simultaneously to sustain and articulate the same pitch;

m. 11, beat 1, RH: the b♮′ of this dyad is possibly the result of a slip of Waller's finger, though he could be attempting to create an ambiguous pitch;

mm. 15–16; mm. 23–24: the second of each of these pairs of measures should be played as an echo of the first;

m. 21, beat 3, RH: the triplet embellishment is at best faintly audible only when the recording is played at half speed;

m. 29, beat 3, RH: for this beat only, the eighth notes are swung;

m. 37: RH, even eighth notes; LH, swung eighth notes;

m. 38: this measure is rendered in real time ($\frac{9}{8}$, or 3+2+4 over 8) to provide an accurate description of Waller's performance; Waller's intention was certainly to stretch the beats, however, not to change the meter; conceptually, mm. 35–41 are the equivalent of the eight-measure A phrase;

m. 40, beat 2, RH: though almost inaudible at full speed, Waller's articulation of the thirty-second note f″ can be clearly heard at half-speed;

m. 42: without changing the speed of the sixteenth-note pulse or the pattern of figuration established in the first beat of m. 42, Waller shifts the accent at the downbeat of m. 43 from the expected c‴ to the actual a″. Thus, m. 42 apparently contains seventeen individual sixteenth notes, rendered as 4 + 4 + 4 + 5 over 16;

mm. 50–51; mm. 52–53: these parallel two-measure phrases (which together constitute the bridge) should be played with a similar pattern of gradually shifting tempi: beginning briskly in mm. 50 and 52 (half note at 76 bpm, as indicated in m. 42), but broadening in beats 3 and 4 of the second measure of each pair (mm. 51 and 53);

m. 51, beat 4, RH: the grace note is played on the beat, almost simultaneous with the quarter-note d‴, the result, possibly, of a slip of the finger;

m. 53: the time signature $\frac{5}{4}$ here (and in m. 59) is used to reflect Waller's expansion of what would have been, conceptually, the fourth beat of a $\frac{4}{4}$ measure; the three sixteenth notes of beat 5, though ostensibly governed by the tempo at the beginning of the phrase (half note at 76 bpm), in practice should equal in value the eighth note of the new tempo cited at m. 54 (half note at 104 bpm);

mm. 54–57: the eighth notes in this passage may sound at first hearing almost even; however, when the recording is played at half-speed, it becomes more apparent that Waller articulates the eighth notes in a subtle swung rhythm pattern;

m. 59, beat 4: swung eighths;

m. 60, beats 4–5: the b‴ grace note is struck simultaneously with each c⁗, but released almost instantly while the octave is sustained a fraction of a second longer;

mm. 85–86: the meters designated in the transcription of these two measures ($\frac{11}{8}$ and $\frac{9}{8}$) are intended to reflect the actual rhythmic configuration of Waller's performance; that is, the eighth note is the unit of pulse and all eighth notes are played evenly and have equal value; it does not suggest Waller's conception of the phrase, which is much more likely to be in $\frac{4}{4}$ time;

m. 88, beat 3, RH: it is possible that the b♮′ is a slip of the finger, but Waller plays it authoritatively, suggesting that it is intentional;

mm. 89–104: the metronome marking of half note at 162 bpm is accurate; despite this breathtakingly fast pace, Waller plays this passage with astonishing precision and clarity; the pedal is not used until m. 102;

m. 106: it is conceivable that Waller intended m. 106 to share the rhythmic profile of m. 105 (note also that the three similar gestures of mm. 111–13 are all consistent with the pattern of m. 105);

m. 107: it is difficult to establish precisely the rhythmic profile of this measure; in real time, it appears to share the profile of m. 106. Played at half speed, however, there is the suggestion of a repeated chord (a pattern identical to that of m. 105), though this may also be the effect of an echo in the recording;

m. 114: as in mm. 105–7, Waller may have intended the rhythmic profile of m. 114 to mirror that of the three previous gestures; indeed, played at real time speed, it is possible to detect an echo of the G^7 chord on beat 2 that suggests such consistency; however, at half speed, the echo is no longer evident;

m. 115: the glissando begins directly on the second beat and lasts 3 1/2 beats;

m. 124, beats 1–2: the tenuto lasts approximately 4 beats;

m. 124, beats 3–4: the tenuto lasts approximately 5 beats;

m. 128, beat 3: the RH f anticipates the LH FF by an almost imperceptible degree; given that this constitutes Waller's final moment of signifying on the style of European nineteenth-century virtuoso piano music (see Introduction: Parody), his intention would probably have been to strike the two pitches simultaneously.

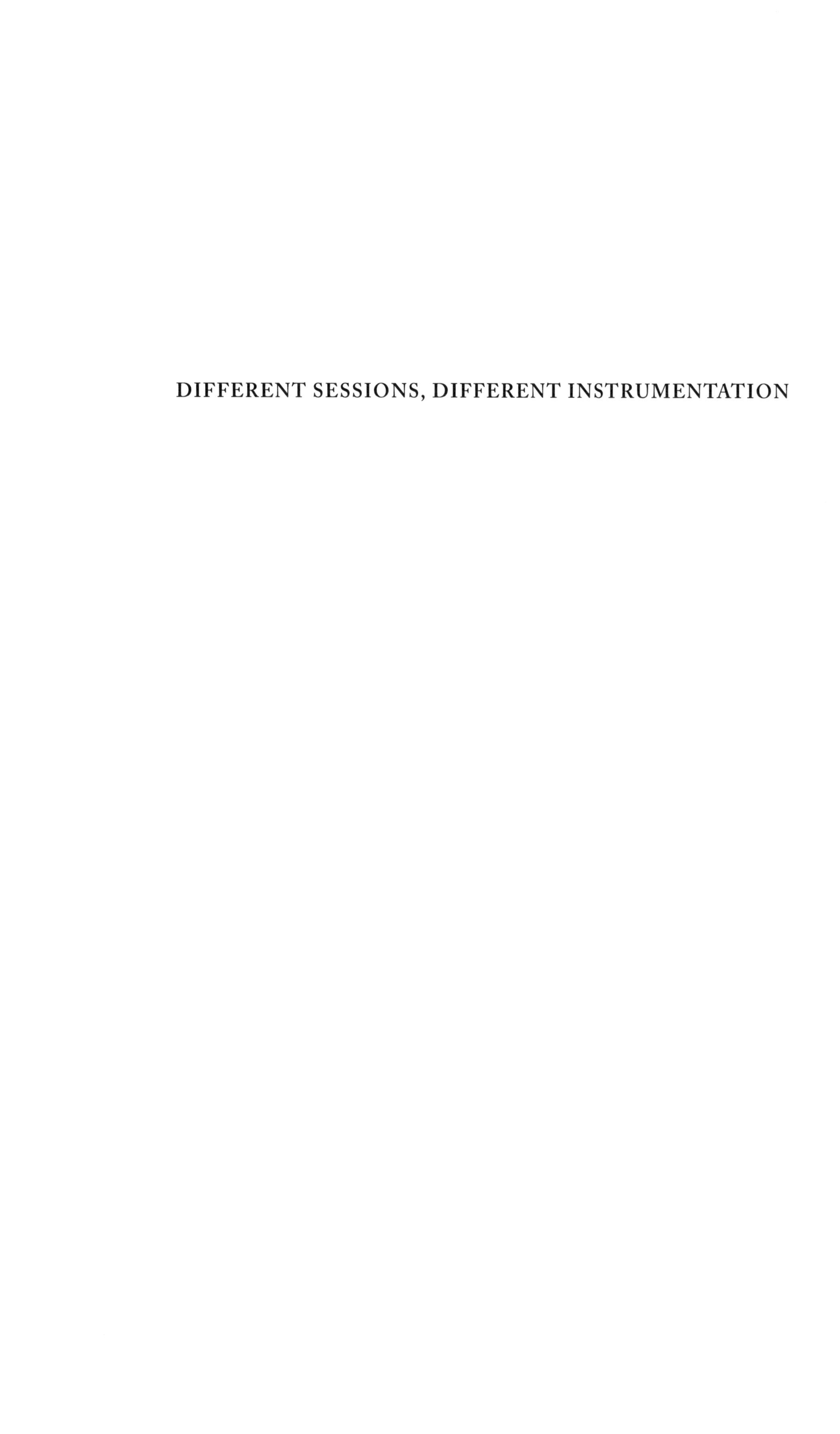

DIFFERENT SESSIONS, DIFFERENT INSTRUMENTATION

7. AIN'T MISBEHAVIN'

Music. Thomas "Fats" Waller (& Harry Brooks[1])
Lyrics. Andy Razaf
Copyright. EP 8110 (8 July 1929)

"Ain't Misbehavin' " is not only one of Waller's most enduring and popular songs,[2] it is one of his most elegantly constructed as well. The A phrase of the AABA chorus divides into two equal half-phrases which mirror each other in terms of harmonic motion, progressing in the first half-phrase (four measures) from tonic to subdominant and then, through a turn to the minor subdominant, relapsing in the second half-phrase back to the tonic (see Transcription 7a). Waller reinforces this harmonic balance melodically by recapitulating the first two measures of the melody in the second half of the phrase, concluding with a single sustained pitch. The melody unfolds in short, parallel gestures each ending in an upward leap of a fourth or fifth, rising through three iterations to a climactic high point in the fourth measure. Thereafter, it begins again on the tonic and comes to rest on the mediant after two measures. The bridge or B phrase contrasts with the A phrase harmonically by beginning in the relative minor, yet it also shares with the A phrase a divided shape of two balanced halves. A pedal on the submediant stabilizes the progression in the first half of the phrase, while in the second half, the harmony prepares for the return to the tonic with a V^6_4–V/vi–vi–V/V–V progression. A repeated descending third, c‴–a″—the simplest of motives—serves as the sole melodic material for the first half of the bridge, while the line for the second half, a stepwise descent of a fifth, is likewise economical in design. Both the A phrase and the bridge, then, manifest a curve of tension that rises to the middle of the phrase and subsides over the second half of the phrase; and, importantly for Waller as a performer, each is readily adaptable to improvised embellishment, melodic variation, and harmonic substitution.[3]

---

[1]Though Brooks's name shares credit with Waller's as composer, it is likely that this is only for purposes of copyright.

[2]Among Waller's output, only "Honeysuckle Rose" can match it in number of recorded performances prior to the 1942 recording ban.

[3]For a more detailed discussion of the construction of "Ain't Misbehavin'," see Paul S. Machlin, *Stride: The Music of Fats Waller* (Boston: Twayne Publishers, 1985), 26–30.

7a. AIN'T MISBEHAVIN'

Recorded 2 August 1929 (mx. 49492-3)

Words by
Andy Razaf

Music by
Thomas "Fats" Waller
and Harry Brooks

mp
3
[Ped. *]
cresc.
mf
3
Ped. *
Ped. *
f
Ped. *
Ped. *
Ped. *
Ped. *
p
Ped. Ped. Ped. *

mp
[Ped.
Ped.
cresc.
Ped.
mf
f
mf
Ped.]

44
f
mf
f
47
mf
50
f
53
mf
p
f
senza
57
mp
p
3

60
63
mp
3
cresc.
f
67
mf
f
Ped.
70
mf
73
[Ped.]
Ped.
[Ped.
Ped.]
76
[Ped.
Ped.
Ped.]

mp
cresc.
f
mf
f

mf
[Ped. ✻]
f
Ped.
✻
†
††

109
[Ped. Ped.] Ped. * [Ped. * Ped. * Ped. * Ped. *]
112
8
[Ped. * Ped. *] Ped. * Ped. * Ped. * Ped. *
115
(8)
Ped. * Ped. * [Ped. *]
118
(8)
dim.
Ped. * Ped. *
121
8
p
[Ped.]
8

Commentary

Title. Ain't Misbehavin'
Source. Victor 78 rpm
Matrix number. 49492-3
Recording date. 2 August 1929
Reissue. "Fats" Waller, "Complete Recordings," vol. 3 (1927–1929) (RCA 741.076, March 1973, LP)

Performance notes. This performance consists of a six-measure introduction (mm. 1–6), a thirty-two-measure AABA chorus (mm. 7–38, in which the last two measures function as a transitional passage), two eight-measure verse phrases (mm. 39–46, 47–54), a second thirty-two-measure chorus (mm. 55–86, in which the final two measures are altered to become part of a four-measure transition, mm. 85–88, such that the last phrase of the chorus is grafted seamlessly onto the transition), and a third thirty-two-measure chorus (mm. 89–120) in which the last two measures function as part of the six-measure coda (mm. 118–24). Perhaps the most notable aspect of the performance is that Waller's improvisation over the three choruses evolves clearly towards an increasingly abstract interpretation of the tune. In the first chorus, Waller remains quite faithful to the original melody; in the second, he employs only the essential pitches from the line (see especially mm. 55–56); in the third, he pares the tune even further to an absolute minimum (see mm. 88–94). In addition, perhaps to compensate for this reduction in melodic pitch content, Waller uses fuller chords, increases the breadth of his range, and intensifies the percussiveness of his attack. His articulation becomes more sharply accentuated with each succeeding chorus, and in the third chorus he avoids using the damper pedal almost entirely until the bridge.

Critical notes. M. 6, beat 4–m. 7, beat 1, LH: Waller rolls the left hand tenth within the context of a swung eighth-note pattern, beginning with the bass note on the final third of the offbeat and concluding on the upper tenth or chord on the strong (i.e., down) beat;

m. 7, beat 2, LH: it is conceivable, perhaps probable, that Waller actually articulated a chord on this beat in the left hand, and that he simply failed to apply sufficient pressure to the keyboard for the chord to sound; nevertheless, the silence in the left hand creates an elegant moment of monophonic simplicity in an otherwise richly chordal texture that is worth preserving;

m. 23: the dyad on the downbeat sounds for the full four beats of the measure; in order to achieve this sonority, given the disposition of pitches in the measure, use of the damper pedal is required; nevertheless, Waller's articulation of the upper voices is remarkably crisp and clear;

mm. 37–38, beats 1 and 2: although the disposition of pitches between the two hands is slightly different on beat 1 for each of these two measures in the transcription, in both measures Waller stresses the e′ of beat 1 and the d♯′ of beat 2, giving the e′ a somewhat heavier emphasis—an effect similar to an appoggiatura;

mm. 39–40: due to the limited fidelity of the recording, Waller's pedaling is somewhat difficult to establish for this phrase, but m. 40, which has a configuration similar to that of m. 42, could be played with or without the damper pedal, assuming the pianist's hands are large enough to hold the three pitches of the left-hand chord;

m. 39, beats 3–4 to m. 40, beat 1, RH: Waller brings out the rising line in the inner voice (b♭–c′–e♭′);

m. 41, beats 3–4, RH: for the second statement of this two-measure figure, Waller uses a detached articulation of beats 3 and 4, while still maintaining the inner voice of the right hand as the predominant line of the texture (see also mm. 47 and 49);

m. 44, beats 3–4, RH: though similar to the closing gestures of mm. 40, 42, etc., Waller's articulation of this figure here is apparently different; he seems not to emphasize (or sustain) the c♯′, perhaps because in this instance the figure is isolated rather than coming at the end of a chain of such gestures;

m. 52, LH: Waller brings out the descending eighth-note line;

mm. 53–54: the legato articulation may have been enhanced by discreet use of the damper pedal;

m. 57: if Waller uses the damper pedal on each beat, he does so only very briefly.

m. 70, beat 3 1/2, RH: the d′ of this chord is accented;

mm. 71–73, LH: each group of four quarter notes is legato and connected; however, because of the clarity of articulation in the right hand, Waller probably did not use the damper pedal;

m. 75, LH: Waller uses exceptionally legato articulation in the left hand, probably aided by discreet use of the damper pedal;

m. 76, RH: Waller brings out the descending line in the lower voice (f♯″–f♮″–e″–e♭″–d″–d♭″–c″–g′);

mm. 85–89, beat 1, LH: Waller brings out the descending motive in the uppermost voice of the left hand chords of each successive measure;

m. 105, beat 3, RH: the grace note is struck simultaneously with the octave and instantly released;

m. 109, LH: Waller brings out the descending line in the uppermost voice (d′–c′–b–d′);

mm. 109–12: Waller uses legato articulation in both hands, aided by discreet use of the damper pedal on beats 1, 2, and 3 of m. 109, and on beats 1 and 3 of mm. 110–12;

m. 113, beat 1; m. 114, beat 1; m. 115, beat 1; LH: Waller stresses the top voice of each downbeat chord in the left hand, creating a descending line of a third (b♭–a♭–g).

7b. AIN'T MISBEHAVIN'

Recorded 11 March 1935
(Muzak Transcription Disk A-273)

Words by
Andy Razaf

Music by
Thomas "Fats" Waller
and Harry Brooks

mp
mf
p
p

28
(8)
mp
30
pp
dim.
senza Ped.
33
mf
No one to talk with, all by my - self, no one to walk with, but
p
36
{I'm hap - py} on ___ the shelf, Ain't Mis - be - hav-in', I'm ___ sav - in' all ___ my l-ove for
39
___ you. Oh, you {hear} me talk - in' {to} ya? I don't stay out late,
f
mp

42
mf
no place to go,
{I'm} home {a - bout eight at my neigh-bor's ra - di - o,}
45
mp
{Ain't Mis - be - hav - in', I'm sav - in' all my love} for
47
you. {Ah,} you dog, you.
49
mf
{Like Jack Hor - ner} {sit}-tin' in a {cor - ner,} Don't go {no-where,

52
what do I care?} Oh, {your kiss - es} are worth {wait - ing} for,
Ped. ❊ Ped. Ped. ❊ Ped. ❊ Ped. ❊
55
mf
ah, buh - lieve me, Don't {stay out late,}
Ped. ❊ Ped. ❊ Ped. ❊
58
f
3
Don't {got} no place to go, {Home a - bout eight at my}
Ped. ❊
60
dim.
mp
5
lit - tle {ra - di - o, and I'm chirp - in', ba - by,} I ain't mis - con-
Ped. ❊

62
- duct - in', I'm sav - in' my con - fec - tion for you. Ha, ha, ha, ha, ha,
64
{yes,} you! (giggle
66
mp
guffaw) Yes, you!
Ped.

Commentary

Title. Ain't Misbehavin'

Source. Muzak-Associated 16-inch transcription disc; with "I've Got A Feeling I'm Falling" and "My Fate Is In Your Hands"

Program / Disc number. A-273

Recording date. 11 March 1935

Reissues. "Fats" Waller (Hitherto Unpublished Piano, Vocal and Conversation), vol. 1 (RCA 730.659, n.d. [ca. 1972–73], LP) and "Oh Mercy! Looka' Here" Fats Waller, His Piano, His Rhythm—1935 & 1939 (HSR 5000-2, 1981, LP)

Performance notes. Waller's program for this disc begins with "I've Got A Feeling I'm Falling" and "My Fate Is In Your Hands"; "Ain't Misbehavin' " is the concluding number. Waller improvises a transition on the piano to connect the second and third songs (unlike the transcription disc performance from this same date for "Honeysuckle Rose," in which he uses a spoken introduction as a transition between numbers). By way of an astonishing deceptive cadence (C7 to a whole-tone sonority on B), he modulates from F major to G major, which in turn serves as the dominant of the new tonic of "Ain't Misbehavin' " (C major). He then launches directly into two statements of the thirty-two-measure chorus, the first for piano solo (mm. 1–32) and the second for piano and voice (mm. 33–64). The final phrase of the second chorus is extended by four measures (mm. 65–68), much of which Waller fills with a stylized stage chuckle. He probably had some time remaining to fill on the disc, not only because he erupts into this humorous nonsense, but also because after the final cadence, he proceeds to improvise an additional closing section for piano solo based on the music for "My Fate Is In Your Hands." (Neither the preliminary transition nor this concluding section are included in the transcription.)

Waller maintains a light, crisp attack throughout both choruses, severely restricting his use of the sustaining pedal. In the second chorus, he avoids embellishments, tricks, and other decorative gestures in the right hand, a strategy especially well suited to the piano's accompanying function. Finally, he varies dynamic levels only within a narrow range, rarely rising above mezzo piano. Within this limitation, however, Waller's shifts can be either gradual (mm. 3–5) or sudden (m. 11).

Like all great jazz singers, Waller manipulates pitch and rhythm with a subtlety that cannot be reflected in conventional notation with precision. Nor can the way he varies timbre and pronunciation be quantified and mapped. Still, in this version of "Ain't Misbehavin' " he uses obvious bent pitches and elisions between pitches sparingly, usually at the beginning or end of a phrase (mm. 37, 60). Also, Waller's singing progresses from a relatively straightforward rendition of the tune in the first phrase to speech-song (*sprechstimme*) for the final line, where he consistently displaces the beat relative to the accompaniment. Indeed, the vocal line at this point is, in terms of its rhythmic structure, essentially independent of the accompaniment.

And, of course, Waller signifies on Razaf's original text for humorous purposes. For example, the original line "I'm home about eight, just me and my radio," with its touch of poignancy about the image of loneliness, solitude, and devotion, is transformed into "I'm home about eight at my neighbor's radio" (mm. 43–44). Thus Waller creates a delightful and somewhat naughty paradox: has he borrowed his neighbor's radio, or is he actually not at home, but at his neighbor's house? And if he has indeed gone next door, is he, after all, misbehavin'?

Critical notes. M. 17, beat 1; m. 18, beat 1; m. 19, beat 1; m. 20, beat 1; LH: Waller brings out the rising chromatic line formed by the downbeat pitch of each measure (e–f–f♯–g);

m. 33 ff.: Waller's voice throughout the recording is noticeably louder than the piano, possibly as a result of microphone placement;

m. 37: for the title phrase, Waller modifies his vocal timbre slightly towards a whisper;

m. 49, beat 4; m. 50, beat 4: in real time, the final quarter note of the vocal line in each of these measures (c′, beat 4) appears to anticipate the beat almost imperceptibly; when the performance is played at half speed, however, the final quarter note of the vocal line in each measure appears to sound on the beat exactly;

m. 55, voice: the timbre for "buh-lieve" is changed to a somewhat deeper register, and the long e vowel is exaggerated;

m. 60, beat 4–m. 61, beat 1, voice: the word Waller uses appears to be "chirpin'," but it could also be "cheepin' ";

mm. 65–66, voice: Waller's laugh—a giggle that explodes into a guffaw—defies description.

8. I AIN'T GOT NOBODY

Music. Spencer Williams
Lyrics. Roger Graham
Copyright. E 377653 (7 February 1916)

On one level, this pair of recordings affords a straightforward opportunity to compare Waller's approach to his two principal keyboard instruments in performances of the same piece. However, the decade that separates the two versions witnessed remarkable growth in Waller's technique and style; thus, it is also important to take into account this crucial temporal difference in examining Waller's overall strategies for interpreting the piece.

For the earlier version on pipe organ, Waller begins by quoting the first eight-measure phrase of the chorus, but follows this with a complete statement of the sixteen-measure verse. By contrast, the piano version proceeds directly to the chorus material after a brief, four-measure introduction. This difference in the structural outline of each performance could conceivably stem from the change between 1927 and 1937 in the way the repertory of popular standards—that is, commercially successful songs—was recorded, due in large part to the sheer number of recordings made of pop tunes.[1] Waller's pipe organ performance was one of eleven recordings of the tune in 1927 alone. At the time of the earlier recording, music for the verse would probably still have been integral enough to the public's (or the recording engineer's) conception of the song that it would have automatically been included in the recorded performance. By 1937, however, recordings of standards normally consisted only of repetitions of a song's thirty-two-measure chorus; thus, Waller probably would have been expected to jettison the verse for the later recording.

In terms of structure, the inclusion of the verse constitutes the primary difference between the two performances. The remainder of both performances consists of two statements of the thirty-two-measure chorus. The pipe organ version also contains a concluding two-measure tag. For the first chorus of the organ recording, Waller establishes a measured, regular pace and outlines the melody in an almost seamless legato articulation, often enhanced by filling in the chromatic steps between the pitches of the melody. He varies this articulation only for a figure that embellishes the otherwise static two measures at the end of the first phrase and for one two-measure segment of

[1]Brian Rust's discography *Jazz Records, 1897–1942* includes no fewer than sixty-three separate dates on which "I Ain't Got Nobody" was recorded prior to the 1942 musicians' union recording ban (p. 1895), establishing it as one of the most frequently recorded titles up to that time.

the second phrase. Throughout this initial chorus, Waller shifts dynamic levels suddenly and by a considerable amount, probably accomplishing these changes with quick fluctuations of the swell pedal. In the second chorus, Waller completely alters the mood, setting a faster tempo and employing crisp staccato articulation. He also makes use of the organ's capability of instantly varying the timbre by playing on a different keyboard. When coupled with a change in register, this technique produces a clear sense of call and response.

Waller adopts a more radical approach for the later piano version. He begins the first chorus with an enriched, but nevertheless close, approximation of the melody for the first phrase. Each successive phrase, however, strays increasingly farther from the original profile by the addition of decorative and rhythmic tricks, as well as registral and textural shifts. For the second chorus, Waller abandons the melody completely, exploring new gestures with each phrase, including reducing the substance of the bridge to a series of syncopated chords in the right hand accompanied by spare, percussive open fifths in the bass. Nothing in the organ version is comparable to Waller's extreme distance from the original in the second chorus of the piano version. Despite the rich variation of the piano version, Waller incorporates one device that functions as a structural link between the two choruses. At the end of the bridge of each chorus, Waller inserts a multi-octave glissando to return to the A phrase. In the first chorus, this glissando rises four and one-half octaves, but in the second, it rises an extraordinary seven octaves before abruptly changing course and descending four octaves; in each instance, Waller executes it with the utmost evenness of tone.

8a. I AIN'T GOT NOBODY

Recorded 1 December 1927 (mx. 40094-2)

Words by
Roger Graham

Music by
Spencer Williams
as performed by Thomas "Fats" Waller

𝅗𝅥 = 51

Manuals

pp mp

Pedals

5

pp

9

mp

13
pp
mp
17
pp
mp
3
21
ten.
ten.
rall.
rit.
pp
mf
pp
ten.
ten.
a tempo
25
mp

29
33
37
pp
mf
pp
41
mf
mp

45
mf
mp
49
53
𝅗𝅥 = 74
pp
57

61
65
69
73

76
79
mp
83
87
senza rit.

Commentary

Title. I Ain't Got Nobody
Source. Victor 78 rpm
Matrix number. 40094-2
Recording date. 1 December 1927
Reissue. "Fats" Waller with Morris's Hot Babies, vol. 2 (1927) (RCA 741.062, October 1972, LP)

Performance notes. For the left hand of the verse and first chorus, Waller uses legato articulation for passages involving stepwise melodic motion (e.g., mm. 1, 9–10, 13–20, 21–22, 23–24, 38–56); otherwise, he plays chords on the beat with a detached, sometimes staccato articulation.

Critical notes. M. 32, beat 3, RH: the second eighth note of this beat (g″) is not articulated, since the key is already depressed and held for the first three beats of the measure; thus, as Waller plays the descending melodic gesture in the upper-register in m. 31–32, it sounds as if he bypasses this pitch; clearly, however, he is simply skipping over the concluding pitch of the descent (g″), since he is already holding down that key;

mm. 39–40, LH: Waller's use of the crescendo pedal (presumably for the swell manual, assuming the left hand is playing that manual as opposed to the Great) brings the melodic gesture in the left hand into prominence;

m. 45, beats 2–3, RH: very close scrutiny reveals a miniscule gap between the two c‴ quarter notes, as if Waller barely articulates them; it is conceivable, however, that these two beats could be transcribed as a half note.

8b. I AIN'T GOT NOBODY

Recorded 11 June 1937 (mx. 010656-1)

Words by
Roger Graham

Music by
Spencer Williams
as performed by Thomas "Fats" Waller

17
pp
5
5
p
senza Ped.
Ped.
Ped.
19
tr
3
mf
mf
p
22
25
gliss. (white note)
28

tr
p
8
Ped.

(8)
3
cresc.
p
mp
mf
Ped.

56
59
gliss. (white note)
62
15ma
65
poco rit.
67
rit.
(l.v.)

Commentary

Title. I Ain't Got Nobody
Source. Victor 78 rpm
Matrix number. 010656-1
Recording date. 11 June 1937
Reissue. "Fats" Waller Memorial, vol. 1 (RCA 730.570, 1969, LP)

Critical notes. M. 1, beats 1–3: there seems to be a brief moment of electronic distortion accompanying the opening fifth in the left hand, beyond even what might be expected from 1937 technology; this aspect of the sound, coupled with the sudden diminuendo that follows on beats two and three, suggest that the decline in volume was accomplished electronically in the recording process rather than through Waller's playing; it is possible that the recording level had been set too high, such that the strength of Waller's accent on the opening fifth was unexpected; if so, the recording engineer would then have responded quickly by turning the recording volume down, though possibly overcompensating for the accent in the process; it is also possible, however, that the recording reflects Waller's playing precisely, including the wide range of dynamic level incorporated into the opening measure;

mm. 5–15: the countermelody in the left hand generally constitutes the most prominent voice in the texture;

m. 20, beats 3–4: the left hand is somewhat more prominent than the right hand;

m. 27, beats 2–4, RH: the glissando is played evenly, reaching d″ on beat three and a‴ on beat four;

m. 31, beats 2–4: the right hand is somewhat more prominent than the left hand;

m. 48, beat 3–m. 50, beat 4: though apparently played without use of the damper pedal, Waller nevertheless achieves an exceptional legato articulation in this passage;

mm. 65–67, beat 3: despite Waller's use of a somewhat percussive articulation of the repeated gesture in the right hand, and despite its resulting clarity, the legato in the left hand suggests that he pedaled regularly on beats one and three; still, the pedaling of this passage is difficult to decipher; it is possible Waller may not have used the damper pedal at all.

HOMEMADE ACETATE

9. THAT DOES IT

Music. Attributed to Thomas "Fats" Waller by volume editor
Lyrics. Unknown
Copyright. Waller estate and Wesleyan University; not filed with Library of Congress

Waller may have recorded this disc (together with others of music for his last Broadway show, *Early to Bed*) in order to provide the show's lyricist, producer, or the actor who was to sing the song with a convenient performance of the music for reference. It is also possible that he made all the acetate discs of *Early to Bed* songs for reasons of his own, either for pleasure or to have a fixed version on record. In any case, Waller probably cut the disc around the time that dialogue and individual songs for the show were being stitched together, or perhaps later, when the show would already have been in rehearsal but was still being revised and adjusted.

The aural fidelity of the original acetate cannot have been very high. At the beginning of the performance, there is a spiraling rise in pitch, suggesting that the machine was still winding itself up to recording speed after Waller had begun playing. Although the recorded performance plays in E major, Waller drafted all the preliminary sketches for this song in the key of F major, and the editor has therefore chosen to transcribe "That Does It" in F major. (One may reasonably assume that at some point in the playback/re-recording process, the speed of the recording was slowed just enough such that the original key of the performance sounds one half-step lower than played.) Finally, there is a significant amount of distortion throughout the recording and the overall sound is muffled, lending a hazy, almost surreal quality to the music.

For the first chorus, Waller provides a straightforward, unembellished rendition of the melody. For the second, he creates a stride version. (Because the quality of the recording is poor, it is often impossible to determine with precision the constituent pitches of chords in the left hand for the second chorus; hence, the editor has placed brackets around the left-hand notes of mm. 44–65 to reflect this ambiguity. The pedaling is likewise difficult to decipher.) There is almost no variation in tempo throughout the recording. A comparison among the sketches and Waller's recorded performance reveals several refinements (see Introduction: Waller's Compositional Process).

9a. THAT DOES IT

(Homemade Acetate Recording, ca. February 1943)

Music by
Thomas "Fats" Waller

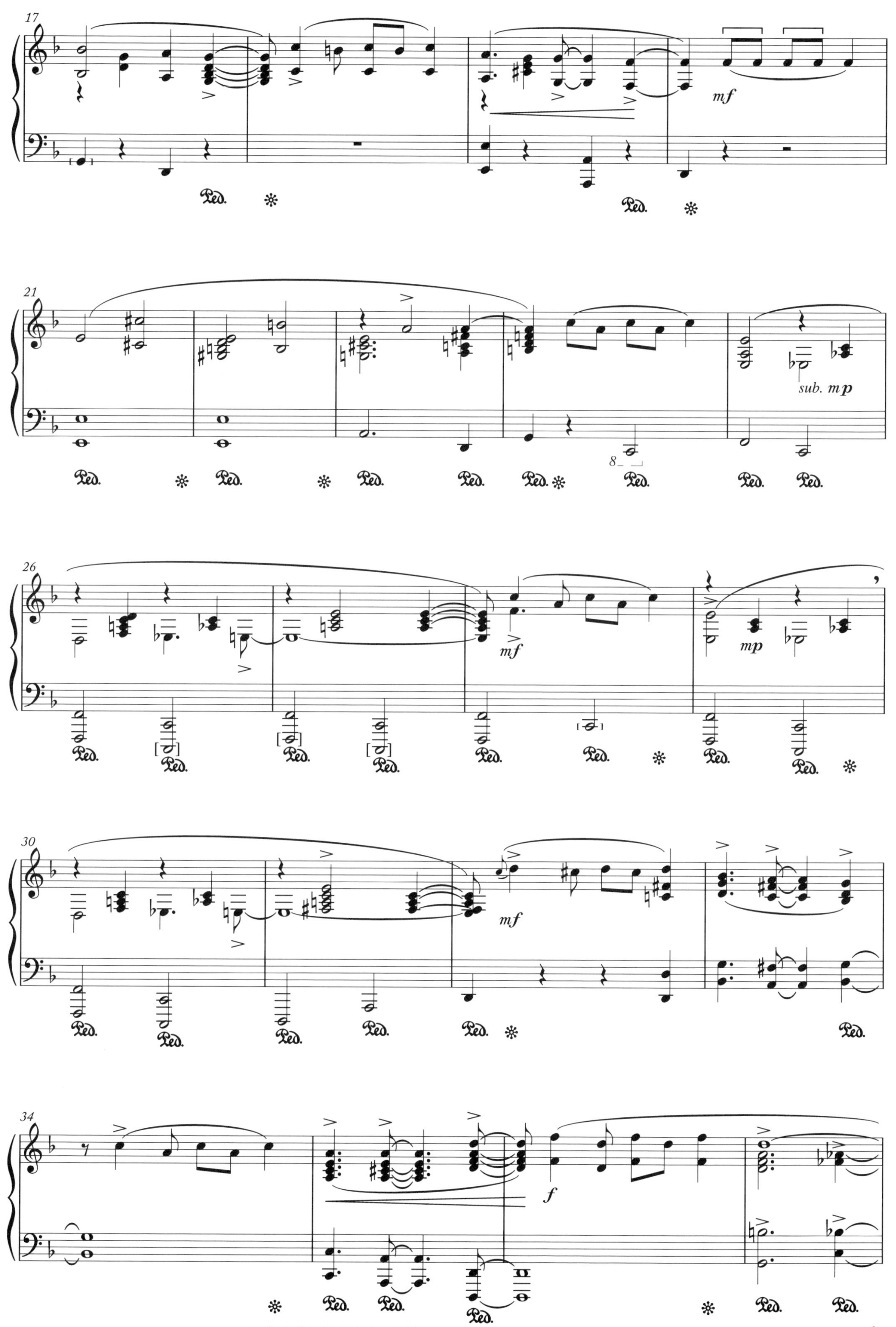
17
mf
Ped.
21
sub. mp
26
mf
mp
30
mf
34
f

38
43
47
51
55

dim.
mf
mp
dim.

Commentary

Title. That Does It

Source. 1/4-inch reel-to-reel tape of homemade acetate recording (Clifford Morris Collection of tapes made by Ed Kirkeby; World Music Archives, Olin Library, Wesleyan University)

Matrix number. None

Recording date. Probably February 1943

Reissue. None

Critical notes. M. 5, beat 3, RH: the a″ on the second eighth note of this beat is probably the result of a finger slip;

m. 51, beat 3, RH: the grace note is played almost simultaneously with the pitch b″; it is possible that this was the result of a slip of the finger;

m. 54, beat 1, RH: it is possible that the b′ is the result of a finger slip, but given the vacillation between c and b in the rest of the measure, it seems equally likely that Waller intended this octave/dyad to be played as notated;

m. 60, beat 3, RH: the dyad on the second eighth note of this beat is probably not a finger slip;

m. 62, beats 3–4, LH: Waller attempts a new progression here, confirming his willingness to experiment in performance even in the details of harmonic construction.

APPARATUS

Sources

Recordings used for the individual transcriptions printed in this edition are listed in the critical commentary that follows each transcription. More generally, the history of Waller's performances on record had an important influence on the genesis of this volume. In 1969, the French subsidiary of RCA Records (RCA France) issued a boxed set of five LP discs containing seventy-two takes of different titles recorded by Waller, originally issued as 78 rpm discs for Victor. The set was titled simply *"Fats" Waller Memorial* and surveys his twenty-one year career as a recording artist. This was followed in 1971 by a second boxed set of seventy reissued takes (*"Fats" Waller Memorial No. 2*). Unlike the first set, the second contained numerous alternate and previously unissued takes. Then, beginning in 1972, RCA France undertook the ambitious task of reissuing on LP all of Waller's remaining Victor recordings archived in the RCA vaults, including all the alternate and unissued takes that could be located by producer Jean-Paul Guiter. Between the release of the *Memorial No. 2* set and the completion of the project in 1978, a total of twenty-six LP discs was released: twenty-three of these surveyed Waller's Victor recordings chronologically (omitting only those takes already reproduced on the two memorial sets), a twenty-fourth disc included alternate and unissued takes unearthed since production of the earlier volumes, and two final LPs contained material recorded by Waller for broadcast over the radio. The result of this project was the re-release of a staggering five hundred and fifty-one individual sound recordings, not including the material recorded for radio broadcast on the final two discs. Those LPs contain reissues of a total of twelve transcription discs, each of which includes two, three, or four separate songs.

Since the completion of the RCA France project, other Waller material, especially previously unreleased air-checks, has surfaced on LP discs. The labels of these LPs range from the obscure (e.g., Collector's Classics), which typically include no discographical information or notes, to mainstream (e.g., EMI, Biograph). Dan Morgenstern, director of the Institute of Jazz Studies at Rutgers University in Newark, New Jersey, produced the most thorough and useful collection, providing complete discographical information and carefully edited liner notes. This compilation is a three-disc set released on Honeysuckle Rose, a label created only for that set. (It should also be noted that some of Waller's recorded work, principally studio recordings rather than air checks, continues to be reissued in compact disc format; apparently, his music is still appealing.)

An additional source of recordings used for this volume is a set of reel-to-reel tapes bequeathed by Clifford Morris to the World Music Archives of Wesleyan University's Olin Library in Middletown, Connecticut. These tapes were made between 1949 and 1951 by Ed Kirkeby, Waller's last manager, whose goal was to organize and preserve all of Waller's recorded output. Kirkeby included everything he could find: all the commercial 78 rpm recordings (issued as well as unissued takes), sixteen-inch Langworth transcription discs,[1] V-Discs,[2] test pressings, and, most significantly, a group of approximately thirty homemade 78 rpm acetates made available to him by Anita Rutherford Waller, the pianist's widow. The acetates apparently were produced on a personal recording lathe or portable record cutting machine owned by Waller; some date from as early as 1937, others as late as 1943. In the early 1960s, John R. T. Davies, a British Waller enthusiast, produced an LP album including eighteen of these recordings, some of them painstakingly reconstructed from broken and shattered discs. The performances preserved on the remaining acetates, however, could not be rescued and therefore were never reissued. In any event, because Davies produced only ninety-nine copies of the LP, the reissues appearing on that album have not been generally available. The much more extensive Clifford Morris Collection, which includes dubs (i.e., duplicates on magnetic recording tape) of all the homemade acetate recordings in pristine condition, thus represents a new source for studying Waller's playing late in his career.

Finally, there are two known substantial sources of unpublished material relating to Waller's work as a composer. One, housed in the Institute of Jazz Studies at Rutgers, is the collection of memorabilia assembled by Kirkeby both during and after Waller's lifetime.[3] The second is a collection of music manuscripts in Waller's hand, unearthed in New York City in November 1994. The owner, Victor Amerling, found the documents in his late father's office; he believes the collection may have come into his father's possession in the late 1960s or early 1970s. It includes 102 documents—single sheets and folios of music manuscript paper. Eighty-seven of the documents contain music in Waller's hand, from sketches (brief, four-bar melody fragments, other preliminary jottings, and various stages of revisions) to complete drafts (fully realized melodies and piano scores). The additional fifteen documents in the collection are not in Waller's hand. Most of these are in ink and consist of instrumental parts for arrangements of songs by Waller, some of which may have been arranged by the composer. Although currently in private hands, the Amerling Collection will probably be placed into the archive of the Institute of Jazz Studies at Rutgers University in Newark, New Jersey.

Transcription Method

The process of transcribing Waller's recorded performances for this volume involved writing down the music of a particular performance captured at a specific recording session—that is, notating recorded sound in musical symbols. This process requires deftness of its practitioners, since, as James Dapogny observes in the preface to his edition of transcriptions of Jelly Roll Morton's piano solos, "modern music notation developed largely as a prescriptive system, designed to give performers direction on how to realize a piece in performance."[4] Yet any jazz transcription, because it results

---

[1]Transcription discs were sound recordings manufactured from acetate, measuring from sixteen to twenty inches in diameter. They were recorded in a studio for later use solely by radio stations as independent mini-programs or to fill interludes in regular programming.

[2]See Introduction, note 35.

[3]For a detailed inventory of the contents of this collection, see Paul S. Machlin, "Fats Waller Composes: The Sketches, Drafts, and Lead Sheets in the Institute of Jazz Studies Collection," *Annual Review of Jazz Studies (1994–95),* (Lanham, Md. and London: The Scarecrow Press, 1996): 1–24.

[4]James Dapogny, *Ferdinand "Jelly Roll" Morton: The Collected Piano Music* (Washington, D.C.: Smithsonian Institution Press—distributed by Hal Leonard, 1982), 34. Charles Seeger also discusses the purpose of notation in his article "Prescriptive and Descriptive Music Writing," *Musical Quarterly* 44 (1958): 184–95.

from the attempt to reduce an already existing performance to visual symbols, actually constitutes a descriptive account of the playing. The transcriptions published here are intended to reconcile these two seemingly contradictory agendas: that is, they are meant to provide both an accurate description of what Waller played and a prescriptive document from which others could attempt to reenact Waller's performances.

Achieving the first, descriptive objective of this binary goal requires using modern notation, modified and extended as necessary, even though certain aspects of Waller's performance may resist reduction to visual symbols. In order to fulfill the second, prescriptive objective, the transcriber must produce a document that contains sufficient detail to reflect the nuances of Waller's playing, yet that also avoids excessive visual clutter. Users of these transcriptions, particularly performers, should consider turning to the recordings in order to appreciate fully the subtle rhythmic and pianistic effects Waller achieves. In a sense, the transcriptions may be understood as a guide to the recordings, which themselves constitute only one frozen realization by Waller of a particular tune. There can be no definitive, "canonical" version of a Waller performance, with the possible exception of "Honeysuckle Rose, à la Bach, Beethoven, Brahms, and Waller," since he never played a piece the same way twice. In this sense, this edition constitutes an invitation to performers to make additional editorial refinements in the transcriptions in conjunction with the recordings.

Certain conventions of notation for jazz are reasonably well understood and agreed upon. For example, the practice of using undifferentiated eighth notes to stand for what in performance are actually pairs of "swung" eighth notes (the first approximately twice the length of the second, as if the beat were divided in three rather than two). In addition, deciphering pitch in solo piano jazz does not often present insurmountable problems; where pitch ambiguities occur, they are for the most part created either by relatively low-fidelity recording techniques and poor acoustic environments, or by overtones that tend to obscure the identity of the fundamental note. But Waller animates his piano solos with a vast array of subtle temporal gestures and a variety of delicate grace note patterns that pose significant challenges to the transcriber. Indeed, an impressive range of complexities surfaces with respect to transcribing Waller's singing, involving not only lyrics, pitch, and rhythm, but also timbre, accent, inflection, and even pronunciation. These complexities do not yield readily to conventional representation; thus, the standard manuscript notation for western European music must be supplemented by the addition of symbols devised to represent them (see Notation below). In rendering such details in notation—that is, in reconstructing on the page what was captured on the recording—some editorial bias may inadvertently have been introduced into the transcription.

To minimize that bias in the preparation of this volume, two tools were used to help clarify what Waller played: a tape cassette deck equipped with a half-speed function and variable pitch control, and a computer program (Opcode Systems's *Studio Vision Pro,* version 3.0.1). Each of these devices was used on an ad hoc basis, as necessary. Playing a passage at half-speed enables the transcriber to hear individual pitches from the piano's tenor range to its highest register more distinctly, especially if they are embedded in rapid passagework. By the same token, a bass line can be clarified by setting the tape deck at half speed to make a recording of the relevant passage, and then playing it back at normal speed. In this way the speed of the passage is doubled, pitch is raised one octave, and a more distinct profile of the bass line is achieved. The Opcode computer program, on the other hand, reduces the speed of a recorded excerpt without any concomitant change in pitch. This device was used to help clarify a few rapidly executed passages in the piano's middle range.

It is important that any user of this volume understand that each recording Waller made represents only one possible version of that particular piece. Thus, some features of Waller's playing will be unique to that version; any editorial emendations, even of pitches that can easily be construed as slips of the finger, risk reducing the integrity of the version. Therefore, the editor has sought in these transcriptions to reproduce as precisely as possible on the page what Waller recorded on a given occasion—in other words, to render the jazz equivalent of a diplomatic transcription of a composer's written manuscript. As a result of this approach, each document incorporates information in the form of notation that might seem superfluous, perhaps awkward or cumbersome to play, or simply incorrect. But what at first glance appears to be a slip of the finger, for example, may actually constitute either an intentional embellishment or a coloristic device. Likewise, gestures applied at parallel junctures in a chorus will almost never, in Waller's hands, be identical, either in substance or in articulation; hence the small variants between such gestures may well be intentional. Passages that look awkward on the page or that are difficult to execute have nevertheless been transcribed as heard. Waller's hands could stretch the interval of a twelfth, which he could play without resorting to a roll, and he had remarkably nimble (if large) fingers that he used in service of a formidable technique. In any case, a performer using this volume might wish to emend some of the more complex or intricate figures on the page (shifting slightly the placement of grace notes or rhythmic gestures, for example, or resolving dissonances that may be fairly characterized as slips or wrong notes), in order to render them in a cleaner and more readily playable form.

Transcribing the ensemble and pipe organ recordings entails addressing still other issues. In the ensemble recordings, the volume level of the accompanying instruments is low, occasionally making it difficult to determine pitch as well as the precise rhythmic pattern of a gesture. The double bass part, because of its low register, is particularly opaque. In the pipe organ recordings, establishing Waller's registrations with precision proves a challenging task, not only because of the sound quality of the recording, but also because of the myriad possibilities for stop combinations.

Notation

General

Accidentals

Accidentals introduced into the score are canceled at the end of the measure by the bar line in accord with convention; however, a courtesy repetition or cancellation of a specific accidental may appear as a reminder at the discretion of the editor.

Dynamics

Approximate dynamic indications were first established for each transcription with aid of a handheld decibel meter; these general levels were then edited and refined by the volume editor to reflect more accurately the relative volume levels achieved in each recording.

Measure Numbers

Measures are numbered consecutively throughout each transcription, beginning with the first full measure. Some published jazz transcriptions begin the consecutive numbering of measures with each new section of the piece, using the name of the section (e.g., "Introduction," "Chorus," etc.) and an uppercase letter to identify the particular section. While such a scheme might work well for some of the transcriptions in this volume, for others, given their formal ambiguities ("Honeysuckle Rose à la Bach, Beethoven, Brahms, and Waller" or "Gladyse," for example), this system would have proven cumbersome. In order to be consistent throughout the volume, therefore, a straightforward sequential approach to numbering measures has been adopted.

Pitches

Waller frequently enhances pitches for expressive effect. Symbols used in this edition to capture these effects include:

represents an ascending portamento or continuous glide upward; a pitch in parentheses at the right end of the line (where present) indicates the concluding pitch of the glide, but it is not meant to be sounded explicitly or emphasized;

represents a descending portamento or continuous glide downward; a pitch in parentheses at the right end of the line (where present) indicates the concluding pitch of the glide, but it is not meant to be sounded explicitly or emphasized;

cue-size notes that appear in parentheses within a diagonal line representing a smooth glissando or slide between two terminal pitches are placed at the approximate moment at which the pitch in parentheses sounds, in order to indicate the pacing of the gesture;

represents an ascending portamento or glide up in pitch; appearing at the beginning of a phrase or line, the ascent ends at the pitch at the right end of the curved line; where it appears following a pitch, the symbol indicates an upward swoop in pitch that lacks a definitive endpoint; in either instance, this is a somewhat more loosely inflected elision, briefer and more concentrated in force than that represented by a straight line;

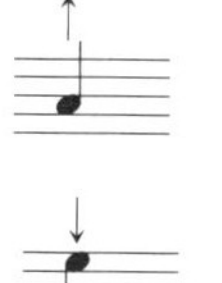

indicates that the actual pitch performed is slightly above notated pitch, but less than a semitone higher;

indicates that the actual pitch performed is slightly below notated pitch, but less than a semitone lower;

indicates a bent pitch; the note is sounded on or very close to the pitch indicated and inflected downward, lowering the pitch less than a semitone;

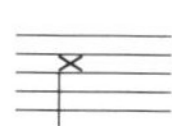

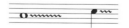

indicates a pitch spoken more than sung; the position of the "x"-note head on the staff indicates the approximate pitch level relative to other spoken syllables;

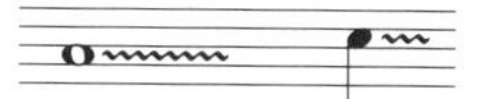

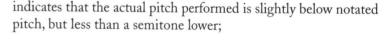

indicates prominent vibrato—an oscillating variation of pitch and intensity used for expressive effect.

Rhythm

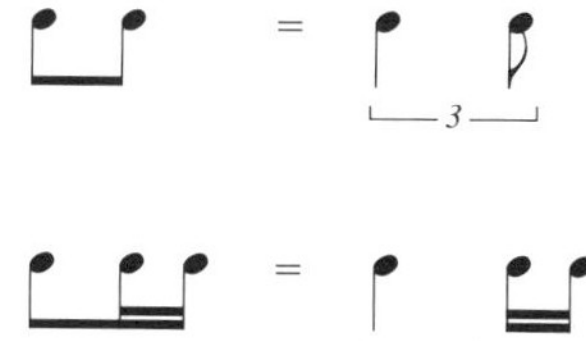

All even eighth notes in this edition should be considered swung unless otherwise marked in accordance with common practice in jazz transcription; in performance the first eighth note of each pair should be lengthened to produce an almost triplet feel. This is also true of other duple divisions of the pulse that include sixteenth notes; however, where the designation "even eighths" appears over

otherwise undifferentiated eighth notes, the eighth notes are to be accorded equal value (i.e., as written). Such straight eighths that appear for just a beat or two are indicated with a horizontal bracket over pairs of eighth notes to show that they should be performed as even eighth notes; in longer passages of notated eighth notes, the designation "swung" may appear over undifferentiated eighth notes to indicate that the swung rhythmic pattern applies at that point until "even" reappears above the score;

an arrow pointing to the left indicates that the pitch is anticipated and should be articulated slightly before the designated note;

an arrow pointing to the right indicates that the pitch is delayed and should be articulated slightly after the designated note.

Tempo

Wherever specified, tempos were determined using a Seiko DM-20 digital metronome and are given in beats per minute (bpm). The speeds indicated are accurate insofar as they match the performance as heard on LP reissue, with minor adjustments in turntable speed made as needed to achieve pitch accuracy. The tempo of Waller's performance measured on an LP reissue may not represent the precise tempo of the original live performance, since at least two transfers in media were involved—live performance to 78 rpm disc and 78 rpm disc to LP disc. But these variations from the original tempo should be negligible.

Although Waller generally maintains a remarkable level of consistency in tempo throughout a chorus and even an entire take, occasionally a slight increase or decrease in tempo can be detected. This small degree of variation should probably be ascribed to flexibility in Waller's playing and is not reflected in the metronome markings in the transcriptions. When the editor felt that a tempo variation was significant enough to represent a change in tempo, this change is indicated above the score. It should be remembered that although Waller kept strict time in his playing for the most part, there is nevertheless a palpable sense of looseness to his beat—a very powerful swing.

Trills

Where the fluctuation between two pitches in any recording is too rapid to be rendered in measured notation, a trill is indicated.

Editorial

Brackets

Brackets surrounding a particular pitch, chord, articulation mark, or passage indicate that the item or music so enclosed presented an ambiguity that could not be fully deciphered or completely resolved to the editor's satisfaction. Thus, notations so enclosed constitute the editor's considered reconstruction of a passage.

Footnotes

Footnotes are used in the transcriptions to suggest alternative renderings of individual items (chords, dyads, grace notes, embellished pitches, etc.) where the transcribed item, in the editor's view, includes a pitch played unintentionally—i.e., as a result of a slip of Waller's finger (see Mistakes below). The user is invited to select from the possible alternatives in these cases.

Mistakes

Where the editor considers it likely that a sound present on the recording may have been unintentional, i.e., a "mistake," a footnote has been provided with a possible alternate reading of the musical text, and the error has been discussed in the critical commentary. Because of the impossibility of assessing the intent of the improvising performer captured on record, the transcription itself represents everything heard on the recording to the best of the editor's abilities.

Mixed Meter

Certain passages were transcribed in mixed meters (see "Honeysuckle Rose, à la Bach, Beethoven, Brahms, and Waller"). Such fluctuation among metrical designations seemed to the editor the most accurate way to represent in notation what Waller played on the recording, helping to capture certain nuances of tempo and flexible time. These meters, however, are not intended to imply that Waller was actually thinking in $\frac{17}{16}$ or $\frac{5}{4}$; rather, the use of such meters constitutes the best notational tool for realizing Waller's rhythmic nuance and his ability to stretch the beat.

Ordering

To facilitate comparison, the transcriptions of the same tune have been organized in pairs and grouped by instrumentation and type. Within each pair the transcriptions appear chronologically. When recordings were made on the same day, they are ordered by matrix or program number. A simple chronological ordering would have produced the following disposition of transcriptions: 2a/b, 8a, 7a, 1a/b, 3a/b, 5a, 5b, 6a, 7b, 8b, 4a/b, 6b, 9.

Song Titles and Attributions

Song titles appear in two formats. On the part titles they are presented as in the copyright registration, while on the transcription and in the commentary, they appear as listed on the recording. Punctuation has been regularized in keeping with standard convention. Attributions appear in the commentary as they appear in the copyright registration, although spelling and orthography have been regularized. Dubious attributions are discussed in the commentaries.

Stemming, Beaming, Ties, and Other Notational Conventions

The notation follows standard conventions and has been used with two priorities: first, to represent the sound of the recording as accurately and precisely as possible, and, second, to help the user appreciate at a glance the melodic, motivic, and harmonic structures of the music.

Articulation

Accent Marks

In his singing and his playing, Waller uses accents to affect the listener's perception of both the melodic and rhythmic profiles of the music. Although the present edition distinguishes between two categories of accent, one could nevertheless argue persuasively that the intensity of Waller's accents in his performances spans a continuum from barely perceptible to exceptionally strong. When used in conjunction with a chord, the accent mark pertains to the pitch it is placed directly above or below. In pipe organ performances, the accent was probably produced by a momentary use of the expression pedal or by the organ's second touch feature (see Appendix). In this edition, the two categories of accent are indicated by the following accent marks:

- > a sharp, percussive accent; a forcefully struck pitch or chord
- – an emphasis that lacks a sharp or percussive articulation; using weight and/or length to achieve prominence in the texture

Commas

A comma in the score indicates a momentary cessation of sound, even though it may appear in the middle of a phrase or beneath a phrase arc or slur line. This kind of miniscule rupture—for example, in an otherwise legato line—is of shorter duration and less fully pronounced than the break produced at the end of a phrase. However, the actual and specific length of the pause indicated by a comma is not represented here.

Fermatas and Tenuto Indications

A tenuto (*ten.*) indicates only a brief extension of the pitch or chord beyond its assigned value; a fermata indicates a lengthy extension of the pitch or chord.

Phrase Arcs

A phrase arc appearing over a vocal line indicates legato articulation; lack of a phrase arc indicates detached and more percussive articulation. In instrumental notation, a phrase arc encapsulates a conceptual unit defined by a breath or realized interpretively through articulation.

Slurring

Slurs have been added to the notation to reflect the articulations heard on the recording. They often reinforce phrasing, as well as the rhythmic feel of swing.

Instrumental

Grace Notes

In the performances transcribed for this volume, Waller uses grace notes in seven distinct patterns, enumerated below. As noted above in the "Editorial Methods" section of this apparatus, these transcriptions are intended to serve both descriptive and prescriptive purposes. However, some of these patterns are so intricate, and applied so flexibly by Waller, that it may be impractical for a performer using this edition to attempt to reproduce them with absolute precision each time they appear. Symbols that have been designed to indicate the execution of grace notes more precisely include:

grace notes without slash marks are articulated before the beat;

grace notes with slash marks are articulated on the beat;

indicates that the grace note is articulated on the beat prior to all pitches in the chord in both hands;

indicates that the grace note is articulated on the beat, prior to other pitches in the following chord, but held over to the identical pitch in the following chord (hence, tied to the identical pitch in the following chord), while the other constituent pitches of the chord are articulated;

indicates that the grace note is articulated on the beat, prior to the individual pitch it embellishes but simultaneously with the other pitches in the chord; the grace note is then released as the embellished pitch itself is articulated instantly thereafter, thus resolving the dissonance originally created by the presence of the grace note in the chord;

indicates that the grace note is articulated simultaneously with all the pitches of the chord it embellishes and instantly thereafter released;

in a group of grace notes embellishing a subsequent pitch, the beat is located at the first slashed grace note in the group; thus, in this example, the first three grace notes are articulated before the beat, the fourth grace note is articulated on the beat, and the fifth is articulated instantly thereafter. Waller's performance here is gestural, more than precise.

Left Hand / Right Hand Indications

Left and right hand indications have not been included in the transcriptions because it is impossible to determine with certainty how Waller performed specific passages; however, the performer will find that certain passages can best be executed by crossing hands.

Organ Registrations

The specifications of the Estey Organ played by Waller (see Appendix) are documented in correspondence between the builder and the builder's agent in Philadelphia. Presumably, by consulting the specifications and by listening to Waller's performances, organists could devise their own solutions to the question of registration for the specific instrument on which they intend to perform. Waller's own choice of registrations would have been influenced not only by the instrument's capabilities, but by the exigencies of the recording process, especially the sensitivities of the microphones used. Although using the new electrical technology, the limited fidelity of Waller's organ recordings and the predominance of eight-foot stops makes deciphering the registrations of his performances impractical. To facilitate the development of a registration plan, the editor has indicated probable shifts in registration or change in manual with an asterisk above the staff. As discussed in the critical commentary, some timbre changes are probably due to a sudden change of octave, rather than a registration change. All other symbols are analogous to those used for the piano transcriptions.

Pedaling Indications

In stride piano playing, the damper pedal is typically depressed on the first and third beats of each measure. Often, however, Waller will anticipate the first or third beat slightly by striking the lowest pitch of the left-hand chord on the second eighth note of a swung pair. This technique is used to capture the sound of the lowest pitch of a chord in the bass register (the tonic pitch, for example, or the mediant pitch of the tonic triad in first inversion) in order to sustain it through the following beat, when the remaining pitches of the chord are played. The use of the damper pedal, by sustaining the lowest pitch of the chord in the bass register, thus helps provide the appropriate harmonic substructure through the subsequent beat. Ultimately, the default principle in performance should be to use the damper pedal to sustain all pitches of left-hand chords on strong beats.

The lack of an asterisk following a pedal indication in a transcription signifies that Waller links successive pedaling actions from one 𝆮 indication to the next, maintaining resonance by leaving the dampers raised between such indications. By contrast, the placement of an asterisk following a pedal indication identifies the moment at which the damper pedal is fully released, thus lowering the dampers onto the strings. Waller's pedaling has important consequences for the sound of a passage. If Waller releases the damper pedal exactly at the second or fourth beat, for example, the sound of alternate beats can be crisp and dry, while if he holds the pedal through a subsequent beat, a richer, more resonant, but somewhat less energetic sound is produced. The drier sound enhances the sense of propulsion and swing in a passage, while the more resonant sound mitigates the passage's momentum. Therefore, wherever practical the editor has chosen to notate the specific placement of Ped. indications and asterisks. The age and fidelity of the original recordings causes some ambiguity to be introduced into the transcription of Waller's pedaling. Wherever such ambiguity could not be satisfactorily resolved, pedal markings have been enclosed in brackets (see Brackets).

Rolled Chords

The constituent pitches of the designated chord are struck individually in a rapid ascending sequence, but the precise rhythmic placement of each individual pitch cannot be determined because of the speed of execution. Where the constituent pitches of a chord are played individually in a rapid descending sequence, a rolled chord symbol with an arrow-head pointing down is used.

Text

Punctuation

Punctuation has been added to the lyrical texts in keeping with standard poetic conventions and in response to Waller's parsing and pacing of the text.

Spelling

Spelling and orthography follow Webster's Collegiate Dictionary (tenth edition) except in cases where the spelling has been modified to reflect distortions of Waller's pronunciation for satiric or comic effect.

Vocal Nuance

Transcribing Waller's renditions of texts presents challenges because of the way that the nuances of his vocal production affect meaning. The following symbols were devised in an attempt to capture much of this interpretive dimension: text appearing between braces { } is growled; underlined text is exaggerated, distorted, or otherwise modified in pronunciation; the use of "x" noteheads indicates spoken (not sung) text; V indicates a glottal stop or hard consonant stop; any consonant followed by an underline symbol indicates that the consonant is extended or voiced for the length of time designated by the length of the underline.

Critical Commentary

To facilitate the use of this volume by performers, critical commentary and other performance notes have been placed immediately following each transcription and do not appear as part of the Apparatus. Each transcription is preceded by an introduction to the tune and a brief discussion of significant points of comparison between pairs of performances. Details of title, authorship, and original copyright are provided as part of this introduction. Current copyright information appears with the transcription itself. Following the notation, the editor provides commentary particular to each transcription, such as the title, source, recording date, and reissues. The performance notes offer suggestions to the performer who might wish to recreate Waller's performance.

The critical notes also clarify points of ambiguity in the transcription and amplify the editor's interpretive choices. Abbreviations used in the critical notes include: m. = measure, mm. = measures, LH = left hand (by convention, the lower piano or middle organ staff) and RH = right hand (by convention, the upper piano or organ staff). The lowest organ staff is identified as "pedal." Other indications are not abbreviated: piano, organ, voice, Waller, Carlisle, etc. The octave of a pitch is indicated by the system CC–C–c–c′–c″–c‴ in which c′ is middle C. Each critical note follows the same format (measure number, beat number, staff identification: comment). For example, the note "m. 87, beat 1, RH: the grace note appearing within the first beat may have been intended by Waller as a way of coloring the open octave on the downbeat, but it may also have been a mistake;" tells the user that in measure 87 of the transcription in the right hand (i.e., upper piano staff), the grace note on beat 1 may have been sounded as an unintentional slip of Waller's finger or it may represent an intentional coloration.

APPENDIX

Estey Opus 2370 Pipe Organ

General Description

In the early 1920s, the Victor Talking Machine Company purchased the deconsecrated Trinity Church building located at 114 North 5th Street in Camden, New Jersey; the company's executives had apparently been impressed with the church's acoustics and its potential as a recording studio. The original organ (Opus 1859), a two-manual instrument built in 1921 by the Estey Organ Company of Brattleboro, Vermont,[1] remained in good condition. Since Victor intended to use the studio organ to record a wide variety of music, including orchestral, choral, and operatic as well as popular, the company contracted with the original builder to rebuild and modernize the instrument. These modifications, which included the addition of a third manual, were completed by the Estey Company during the first half of 1925, and further additions and corrections were carried out in May 1926. As a marker of the comprehensiveness of these changes, a new number, Opus 2370,[2] was assigned to the rebuilt instrument—now not a church organ, but an orchestral organ heavily influenced by theater instrument design. The Opus 2370 was then likely one of the most advanced instruments of its type available at the time. The instrument had three manuals (keyboards) and a pedal board coupled to a range of thirty-three ranks of pipes or "stops," each with a characteristic tone color or timbre.

Specifications

The general specifications for the Estey Opus 2370 given in table 1 are cited in letters from G. S. Boyer, the Estey Organ Company's representative in Philadelphia who negotiated the organ's redesign contract with Victor Talking Machine Co. recording engineers.[3] The letters, dated 20 January 1925 and 30 January 1925, are addressed to

[1]The firm was founded in 1846 and purchased two years later by Jacob Estey (1814–90). In 1901, a new pipe organ department opened in Brattleboro under the supervision of William E. Haskell (1865–1927), one of the most gifted inventors in modern organ design.

[2]David L. Junchen, in his *Encyclopedia of the American Theatre Organ,* 2 vols. (Pasadena, California: Showcase Publications, 1985), 2:112–13, gives the Victor organ a third opus number—2529. This later number represents the organ after a second 1926 rebuild. Junchen gives no detail about these modifications, however, and a check of the Estey archives (see note 3) reveals no additional information to support or contradict Junchen's information. For the purpose here, the organ will be identified and described as it is in the Estey correspondence.

[3]The complete records of the Estey Organ Company, including the letters cited here, are held at the Brattleboro Historical Society and Estey Information Center in Brattleboro, Vermont.

Table 1. General specifications for Estey Opus 2370 pipe organ

- twenty universal pistons affecting all manuals, couplers, and pedals
- the usual complement of couplers, given a three manual organ
- two expression shoes of five points each, and a master switch so that both of these shoes can be operated off one shoe
- second touch for the Great and Pedal manuals (see below)
- snare drum, playable on the first touch of the Great
- roll, playable on the second touch of the Great
- bass drum, playable on the second touch of the Pedal
- gong and bird whistle, operated by a pedal piston

Col. J. G[ray] Estey, president of the company from 1902 to 1930, in Brattleboro, Vermont. The compass of the three large manuals is provided as C to c'''' (two octaves below middle C to three octaves above), totaling sixty-one keys. The compass of the pedals is given as CC to g (three octaves below middle C to a fourth below middle C), or thirty-two keys. The letters also provide a complete list of the instrument's thirty-two stops (see table 2).

Second-touch Feature

The Opus 2370 included a "second-touch" feature that allowed the performer to depress the keys about one-eighth of an inch beyond their normal stopping point. Doing so closed an additional electronic circuit that added extra pipes to those already sounding. Normally, an organ would be incapable of responding to the performer's style of attack on the keyboard, but this feature, invented by the British Theater organ specialist Robert Hope-Jones, could be linked to a variety of effects allowing for the instantaneous alteration of timbre. This feature was especially useful to a performer such as Waller as it facilitated loud accents and dramatic shifts of tone color.

TABLE 2. List of organ stops for the Estey Opus 2370 pipe organ

	Name of Stop	Size
Great Organ		
	Major Open Diapason (new)	8 ft.
	First Open Diapason	8 ft.
	Second Open Diapason	8 ft.
	Major Flute (new)	8 ft.
	Flute	8 ft.
	Gamba	8 ft.
	Gemshorn	8 ft.
	Viol d'Orchestre	8 ft.
	Viol Celeste (new)	8 ft.
	Flute	4 ft.
	Flute Harmonic (new)	4 ft.
	Oboe	8 ft.
	Cornopean (new in place of trumpet)	8 ft.
	Clarinet	8 ft.
	Saxophone	8 ft.
	Vox Humana	8 ft.
Swell Organ		
	All stops duplexed from Great, with the addition of a Tremulant stop that produced a tremolo effect.	
Solo Organ		
	Stentorphone (new)	8 ft.
	Tibia Plena (new)	8 ft.
	Gross Gamba (new)	8 ft.
	Gamba Celeste (new)	8 ft.
	First Violin (new)	III Ranks
	Flute (new)	4 ft.
	Piccolo Harmonic (new)	2 ft.
	Orchestral Oboe (new)	8 ft.
	Tuba Profunda (new)	16 ft.
	Tuba (new)	8 ft.
	Clarion (new)	4 ft.
Pedal Organ		
	Open Diapason (new)	16 ft.
	Bourdon (new)	16 ft.
	Bass Viol	8 ft.
	Trombone	16 ft.
	Tuba	8 ft.